KU-299-602

LEEDS BECKETT UNIVERSITY
LIBRARY
DISCARDED

Leeds Metropolitan University

17 0278925 X

Transcultural Management

Transcultural Management

A New Approach for Global Organizations

Atsushi Funakawa

Jossey-Bass Publishers • San Francisco

Copyright © 1997 by Jossey-Bass Inc., Publishers, 350 Sansome Street, San Francisco, California 94104.

All rights reserved. No part of this publication may be reproduced, stored in a retrieval system, or transmitted, in any form or by any means, electronic, mechanical, photo-copying, recording, or otherwise, without the prior written permission of the publisher.

Chapter One epigraph (p. 3) is used by permission of FOREIGN AFFAIRS (Summer 1993). Copyright 1993 by the Council on Foreign Relations, Inc.
Chapter Two epigraph (p. 13) is used by permission of Business One Irwin.
Chapter Four epigraph (p. 37) is from TOTAL GLOBAL STRATEGY by Yip, © 1985. Reprinted by permission of Prentice-Hall, Inc., Upper Saddle River, NJ.
Chapter Five epigraph (p. 49) is reprinted by permission of John Wiley & Sons, Inc.
Chapter Seven epigraph (p. 82) is from Glen Fisher, *Mindsets*, and is reprinted with permission of Intercultural Press, Inc., Yarmouth, ME. Copyright 1988.
Chapter Eight epigraph (p. 99) is used by permission of Richard Pascale.
Chapter Nine epigraph (p. 123) is reprinted by permission of Warner Books, Inc., New York, USA. MEGATRENDS by John Naisbitt. Copyright 1982. All rights reserved.
Chapter Ten epigraph (p. 136) is from *Kaisha: The Japanese Corporation* by James C. Abegglen and George Stalk, Jr. Copyright © 1985 by Basic Books, Inc. Reprinted by permission of BasicBooks, a division of HarperCollins Publishers, Inc.
Chapter Eleven epigraph (p. 150) is from POWER SHIFT by Alvin Toffler. Copyright © 1990 by Alvin Toffler and Heidi Toffler. Used by permission of Bantam Books, a division of Bantam Doubleday Dell Publishing Group, Inc.
Chapter Fourteen epigraph (p. 185) is from Quantum Healing Workshop, Deepak Chopra, M.D., and is used with permission.

Substantial discounts on bulk quantities of Jossey-Bass books are available to corporations, professional associations, and other organizations. For details and discount information, contact the special sales department at Jossey-Bass Inc., Publishers (415) 433–1740; Fax (800) 605–2665.

For sales outside the United States, please contact your local Simon & Schuster International Office.

Jossey-Bass Web address: http://www.josseybass.com

 Manufactured in the United States of America on Lyons Falls Turin Book. This paper is acid-free and 100 percent totally chlorine-free.

Library of Congress Cataloging-in-Publication Data

Funakawa, Atsushi.
    Transcultural management : a new approach for global organizations / Atsushi Funakawa.
        p.   cm. — (The Jossey-Bass business & management series)
    Includes bibliographical references and index.
    ISBN 0-7879-0323-X
    1. International business enterprises—Management.   2. Industrial management—Cross-cultural studies.   I. Title.   II. Series.
HD62.4.F858   1997
658'.049—dc21   97-26466

FIRST EDITION
HB Printing   10 9 8 7 6 5 4 3 2 1

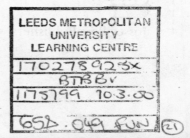
LEEDS METROPOLITAN
UNIVERSITY
LEARNING CENTRE

170278925x
BTBBv
1175799 10·3·00

658·049 FUN   (21)

The Jossey-Bass
Business & Management Series

Contents

Communicate

Part Three: The United States and Japan

Part Four: Moving Forward Across Cultures

Communication →

Dedicated to the memory of my father

Preface

Globalization is not a fad but an inevitable trend for the twenty-first century. More businesspeople and organizations are being exposed to cross-border business than ever and play key roles in today's global economy. However, beneath the surface of globalization, we see many individuals and organizations facing the emerging new challenge of working in the multilingual, multicultural, and multinational environment. Working across borders requires us to work effectively across cultures and languages.

Transcultural Management focuses on how individuals and organizations manage and eventually transcend cultural differences in global business situations. This book provides a framework for doing this within the transcultural management model as a new synthesis of cross-cultural perspectives and management skills. Although the transcultural management model may apply to any cross-cultural business situation, this book focuses on U.S.–Japan organizational issues. By showing that individuals and organizations with significant cultural differences, such as the Americans and the Japanese, can collaborate across cultural boundaries, we can see the durability of transcultural management that leads organizations to be truly global.

The Information Gap

"Baka Yamero!" ("Don't be silly. Forget the idea!") Such were my former boss's first comments when I told him that I was writing a book. He continued, "You are too young to write a book. Don't embarrass yourself."

"That's great. You have a lot of good experience. Write something new. I'm fed up with all the *gaijin* (outside person, foreigner) expert books." Such were the comments from a former graduate school classmate, an American who had lived in Japan.

Being Japanese, I have had qualms about describing what I have experienced and learned and about giving advice to my clients. Thus, the warning from my former boss also reflects my own occasional inner voice. However, I have realized that such a reticent mindset prevents the Japanese from actively participating in global organizations. At the same time, this mindset contributes to an information gap between Japan and other countries, especially the United States. This gap, in turn, reinforces an inaccurate portrayal of Japanese business practices and prevents the two countries from achieving mutual understanding.

According to the survey report, *Supplying Information and Data on Contemporary Japan to the United States,*[1] the information-flow imbalance between the two countries is caused by both the language barrier and the tendency of the Japanese to be extremely reticent—to withhold explanation and expressiveness. In the United States, the tendency is often much the opposite. Consequently, in the past several years, U.S. bookshelves have been stacked with books about Japan and Japanese business practices, most of them written by American scholars or former expatriates. But it is hard to find one written by a front-line Japanese businessperson.

Furthermore, the authors of these business books are often trapped by a cross-cultural communication gap. While outside researchers usually provide a more objective perspective and analysis than those who work inside an organization, if the researchers are not aware of subtle cultural variables and different communication styles, they may not bring to light important information. Quite often, their very observations are a demonstration of typical cross-cultural miscommunication problems. Kichiro Hayashi, a Japanese trailblazer in the field of cross-cultural management, confessed that as an outside researcher he had a difficult time interviewing Japanese managers working for major Japanese companies because he did not have the techniques for adjusting his communication style appropriately.[2] If Japanese researchers have such difficulty, what chance is there for American researchers, who, in most cases, do not speak the language? In addition, American management traditionally analyzes an organization from the top and from the outside. But in a society as cohesive as Japan, an organization may look totally different if it is viewed from the bottom and from the inside.

The Gap Between Hard and Soft Orientation

Working in the area of cross-cultural management, I have come to realize that there is a fragmentation of people, fields, and perceptions within the worlds of business and academia and between "hard" (business-oriented) and "soft" (culture-oriented) individuals. Strategic consultants and financial officers are often categorized as hard, while organization development consultants and human resources managers are labeled as soft. Few experts can go beyond their boundaries. Management gurus and linguists and communication specialists have seen themselves as almost mutually exclusive. Although businesspeople have begun to realize that communication is at the heart of the core competencies in today's information-centered, interdependent economy, few management experts pay attention to the quality of communication. On the other hand, cross-cultural specialists often compare communication styles in the United States and Japan, but they rarely address the attendant implications for corporate strategy.

This fragmentation among disciplines, fields of expertise, and people leads to the separation of culture and business. As a result, it is difficult to provide solutions for people who are dealing with the clashes between cultures.

The Position of This Book

Culture has been mistreated. It has been used to blame others and has often become an excuse for not taking action. Conventional cross-cultural training programs, which stress situations such as how to exchange business cards, do not adequately respond to the needs of today's businesspeople. What is needed are concrete applications for specific business situations, such as conducting a cross-cultural business meeting with an alliance partner. Although it is important to learn, for example, not to send a clock as a gift to a Chinese person (because it implies death), in today's global work environment we have to go beyond a simple list of dos and don'ts for a specific country.

In the 1980s, many companies tried to enter the global marketplace. After establishing local operations, making products accessible to overseas customers, and developing strategic alliance partners, these companies realized that the real challenge had only just begun: the challenge of managing people across cultures. At the dawn of the new century, we can see companies competing to transform themselves into truly global, geocentric organizations. To do this, people have to transform their own mindsets, from ethnocentric to geocentric, from monocultural to multicultural, and eventually to transcultural. This task is not easy. It is only possible if all of us—thinkers and practitioners alike—transcend the boundaries of our particular disciplines and nationalities and work together.

The Audience

Transcultural Management is intended to help all businesspeople in the global workplace, including chief executive officers (CEOs), line managers, and especially human resources managers. The contents of this book are designed to provide integrated views of theoretical frameworks and practical applications for any type of cross-border operation, including overseas branches, strategic alliances, and acquisitions. Most of the chapters contain case scenarios and anecdotes that show clear pictures of cross-cultural management issues, provide frameworks for analyzing the issues, and present recommendations so that managers can practice transcultural management.

Overview of the Contents

This book addresses individual mental models, skill building, and organizational competencies in order to provide specific solution processes for transforming cultural clashes into cultural synergy. Part One (Chapters One through Three) explains how cultural issues affect today's global business practices. Chapter One sets the stage by providing two case scenarios: an American company in Japan and a Japanese company in the United States. Chapter Two explores the impact of culture in today's business organizations and identifies impediments for managers caused by cultural blind spots. Chapter Three focuses on language issues in cross-cultural situations and suggests guidelines so that native English speakers may avoid pitfalls in using English with nonnative speakers.

Part Two (Chapters Four through Eight) provides a theoretical framework of transcultural management and its practices for individuals and organizations. Chapter Four shows the linkage of globalization processes and soft cultural issues and identifies the need for a new strategic cultural intervention for globalizing organizations. Chapter Five outlines the five core competencies of transcultural management that are required of individuals and organizations in the global business arena. Chapter Six identifies the seven mental disciplines that enable individuals to promote the five competencies. Chapter Seven introduces useful models for developing insights on cross-cultural work situations. Chapter Eight examines the theoretical frameworks for managing global organizations and provides a new paradigm: high-context, high-content management.

Part Three (Chapters Nine through Twelve) features specific situations found in the U.S.–Japan cross-cultural business environment. Chapter Nine identifies the root causes of cross-cultural business conflict and describes some issues that are common to Japanese and American organizations. Chapter Ten focuses on the issues of American companies in Japan, and Chapter Eleven examines the opposite situation: Japanese companies in the United States. Chapter Twelve features U.S.–Japan strategic alliances and provides tips for successful alliances. Part Four concludes the book by identifying issues and challenges for those working across cultures (Chapter Thirteen) and provides direction for the future (Chapter Fourteen).

Finally, the Appendix illustrates two practical applications of transcultural management: a global workshop conference and an organizational learning and development project for the cross-border joint venture.

Acknowledgments

Writing a book is not an easy task, especially in a foreign language. However, this hard work was also an enjoyable journey of learning, involving many people and organizations. I'd like to acknowledge two individuals without whom this book wouldn't exist. First, I'm very grateful to Dr. Robert Moran, who not only opened my eyes to the principle of cross-cultural management, but also encouraged me to write a book. Second, I'd like to thank John Kent, who first edited my manuscript and constantly inspired me to new ideas based on his more than two decades of cross-cultural training expertise.

In respect to the learning process, I'd like to thank two teachers in my life. They are, incidentally, two Master Aokis; one is a martial artist, Hiroyuki Aoki, the founder of Shintaido, and the other is a painter, Toshishige Aoki. They both taught me the meaning of learning. I am also very grateful to my classmates at the American Graduate School of International Management, Heidi Joe Faller, Hiroshi Hamada, and Tom Price, who helped me to develop the original idea.

To my former colleagues at Clarke Consulting Group and Geonexus Communications, thanks for your good insights while we were working together. I'm grateful to Dr. Todd Imahori, who continues to share his excellent thoughts linking the practice and concept of intercultural communications. My thanks also to Cliff Clarke, Nadine Kazuko Grant, Bill Grubb, and Robert Moran for reviewing my manuscript.

My deepest thanks to Globis Corporation, which provides the most stimulating, knowledge-creating work environment.

A very profound thank-you to the team at Jossey-Bass. I'm most indebted to Cedric Crocker for agreeing that there was something worth saying about cross-cultural management. My sincere appreciation to Byron Schneider, editor, and Judith McKibben, development editor, for their tireless work.

Finally, special thanks to my wife, Debbie, and my son, Keita, who not only provided constant patience and support but also share a daily cross-cultural experience with me, and to my mom, who has always shown understanding of my cross-cultural learning.

Tokyo, Japan   ATSUSHI FUNAKAWA
August 1997

The Author

ATSUSHI FUNAKAWA is program director of organizational learning and global development at Globis Corporation, a Tokyo-based management development institute. He received his B.A. degree (1980) from Keio University, Tokyo, in law and his Master of International Management (MIM) degree (1991) from the American Graduate School of International Management (Thunderbird).

Funakawa's primary interest is in organizational management and development from a cross-cultural perspective. With his colleagues at Globis, he conducts various cross-cultural organizational intervention projects, particularly for *gaishi* (foreign-capital) companies. These projects include transferring organizational learning programs, codeveloping performance appraisal systems, and facilitating change management. As a frequent speaker, Funakawa has conducted numerous seminars featuring global organizational management from cross-cultural perspectives at organizations and schools on both sides of the Pacific Ocean. He has helped thousands of business professionals from the United States, Japan, Russia, Europe, and Asia. He also teaches transcultural management, organizational behavior, and human resources management at Globis Management School in Tokyo.

Funakawa joined Toshiba headquarters in Tokyo in 1980, where he was trained under Japanese management training systems. In 1983, he joined the Tokyo branch of the American Life Insurance Company, a member company of the American International Group, as a strategic planner. He started his career as a cross-cultural management consultant, first at Clarke Consulting Group, Redwood City, and then at Geonexus Communications, Palo Alto, California. In 1995, he returned to Japan and joined Globis Corporation.

With his American wife, Debbie, Funakawa is raising a bicultural, bilingual son.

Funakawa can be reached at Globis Corporation (011–81–3–5275–3695 or funakawa@globis.co.jp).

Transcultural Management

Part One

The Impact of Culture on Global Business

Chapter One

The Tragedy of Ignorance

*It is my hypothesis that the fundamental source of conflict
in this new world will not be primarily ideological or
primarily economic. The great divisions among humankind
and the dominating source of conflict will be cultural.*
SAMUEL P. HUNTINGTON[1]

In this chapter, we explore critical issues caused by cross-cultural
mismanagement. But first, I would like you to consider the following two case scenarios.

An American Company in Japan

"I have to teach them our way of business," Richard Jones told himself when he was informed of his new assignment as managing director of the Japan branch operation. Until then, he had been the
director of world operations at the New York home office and had
been frustrated with the Japan branch office. It had always seemed
reluctant to cooperate with headquarters, procrastinating over action plans, making excuses because of the "unique" Japanese market and business practices. He had visited the Japan office several
times for business plan review meetings. Not once had he been
able to get clear explanations. He was remembering what the CEO
and president had told him: "Don't waste your time studying Japanese. They should speak English."

Jones's experience after two months in Japan merely con-
firmed his original observations about the Japanese: "The Japanese are not working for us, but for their Japanese customers. That's

why they're insensitive to the time and money we have to spend." So Jones decided to initiate some changes in the Japan branch. He cut the entertainment expenses and the incentive budget for the wholesalers. He also decided that all documents from *kacho* (section managers) had to be written in English. Such strategies, he thought, could improve communication with the Japanese managers. He emphasized an open-door policy and told the Japanese employees to come in and talk whenever they wanted. Despite all his efforts, Jones was still irritated by the Japanese and their seeming lack of initiative. He decided to make a speech at the next board meeting.

Eleven senior Japanese management members were waiting in the boardroom when Jones sat down at the table. He could tell that all the Japanese were politely holding back. "Today, I'd like you to think about something fundamental," he started. "I'd like to ask you a very basic question. Why are we all able to sit here, in this boardroom? Why does this company continue to operate? There is one simple answer to this."

He could hear the echo of his own voice, since, as usual, the Japanese listened in dead silence. He continued, "This company does not exist for the employees, or for the customers, or for the end users, or for our distributors or wholesalers. This company exists for our shareholders, and we are working for them." Looking around at the Japanese faces, he was wondering whether or not they understood. He had noticed before that the Japanese managers didn't really understand what he was saying even though they quietly nodded in apparent agreement. He continued, talking as slowly and clearly as he could. "Without our shareholders, all of you, including myself, wouldn't be here right now; we just couldn't operate. Therefore, it is obvious that we have to fulfill our minimum responsibility to them, which is to make a profit." For the next thirty minutes he reinforced and emphasized the point.

Later that day, Jones ate lunch at the Tokyo American Club. Looking at the small Japanese garden through the window of the dining room while waiting for the meal, he thought about his speech that morning. He felt content. "Now they understand the bottom line," he said to himself. "They should now appreciate the basic laws of capitalism." Meanwhile, Makoto Yamamura, director of marketing, who had attended the board meeting, was talking heatedly to his area marketing managers. "Now it's clear. It's just as I have told you many times. I was right. Those people in New York aren't thinking about us at all. According to Jones, our customers, our wholesalers, are unimportant. All he has in his mind are the shareholders! Even though I couldn't understand everything he said in English, that is the one thing I heard for sure."

Within the next two weeks, this news was transmitted by word of mouth to all the sales branch offices and even to some wholesalers and distributors. In the process, Jones's comments were exaggerated. Some of the distributors called the Japan branch, asking for an apology. Even before this incident, the relationship between the home office and the Japan branch had been strained. The board meeting was the last straw. Within the next four months, three Japanese directors left the company to join competitors, followed by some of the sales agents.

A Japanese Company in the United States

"I'm leaving the company, Mr. Ohta," Michael said to his boss, Yoshihiro Ohta, marketing director of Nakatani USA, Inc., a West Coast subsidiary of the Japanese multinational corporation Nakatani Trading, Inc.

Michael had joined Nakatani USA three months before, after completing an MBA degree in international studies. He was curious about Japanese business and was also attracted by the relatively high salary. He had been to Japan four years previously and had stayed for one year, teaching English to Japanese students. In graduate school, he had taken a Japanese business course and had reached an advanced level in Japanese-language oral communication and an intermediate level in reading and writing. He practiced his self-introduction repeatedly in Japanese and also asked his Japanese friends for help. As a result, at the final job interview at Nakatani USA, he had surprised the Japanese directors, including Ohta, with his knowledge and ability.

Because Nakatani USA dealt with Japanese corporations on the West Coast, it had transferred many Japanese employees to the United States from Japan. The company emphasized the importance of Japanese-language skills when recruiting American employees. They also had what they called "favorable promotion policies" for locally hired Japanese-speaking employees. Given these policies, the five Japanese directors under the CEO of Nakatani USA decided to hire Michael immediately after his final interview. He was assigned to work under Ohta as an assistant marketing coordinator. Ohta, who had a great deal of experience in Japan, had been transferred to the United States one year before and this was his first overseas assignment. Ohta had high expectations of Michael because he assumed that, with his Japanese-language skills, Michael would be one of the few Americans who could fit into a Japanese organization. Currently six other staff members were working under Ohta—five Japanese men from the Tokyo office and one locally hired Japanese American woman working as a secretary.

On Michael's first day, Ohta took him for lunch with his five male Japanese staff members. Michael felt some pressure because he was the only non-Japanese. During lunch, he was overwhelmed with questions, which he had to answer in Japanese. Ohta used only Japanese in the office, although he could speak English quite fluently. He believed that Nakatani USA was a Japanese company and took it for granted that all the employees could speak Japanese. In Tokyo many foreign-capital companies require foreign language skills as the first requirement in recruiting Japanese employees. His daughter was working for a French bank in Tokyo because she could speak French fluently.

After a while, Michael got tired of having lunch with Ohta and the other staff members because they only talked about Japanese issues, mostly related to business. Even so, he decided to meet with them for lunch at least three times a week. He became friends with one of the men, Kenichi Maeda, who was more individualistic than the other four men and did not seem to be satisfied with the status quo. Ohta had been transferred from Tokyo without his family, and he often went drinking with his subordinates after work. Maeda was the only Japanese who did not go drinking with Ohta. One day during lunch with Maeda, the conversation turned to the subject of promotion and work rotation. Michael learned that language ability alone did not guarantee the rapid promotion opportunities he had expected. He was surprised to hear that even for Maeda, who was not locally employed, it would take several years to attain the first managerial position of *kacho*. Although he was disappointed, he thought that he should stay with the company for at least three years in order to get experience, as Maeda had suggested.

Another frustration for Michael was that he could not work independently. The office was laid out Japanese style, and he sat at a cluster of desks with his colleagues. Although Ohta's desk was separate from the others, he could see Michael from where he sat. Quite often, while Michael was working, Ohta watched over his shoulder. Michael became more and more annoyed at being constantly monitored.

Two months after Michael's conversation with Maeda, Ohta decided to hire another local employee. He believed that Michael was satisfied with the working conditions and he appreciated Michael's hard work. Ohta thought it would be a good idea to give him some advice in order to keep him motivated. He called Michael over at the end of the working day, took him into a meeting room, and started: "Listen Michael, we decided to hire another American guy, like you. We will start the recruiting process next week. Before we do, I wanted to tell you something. You will become his *senpai* (more experienced, senior member). You know what that means. Although he is not your subordinate, you will have to teach him all the dos and don'ts. You should take care of this guy as your *kohai* (less experienced, junior member). For instance, you should also offer him advice about choosing an appropriate girlfriend and about his future plans. This is important in a Japanese organization." Ohta continued to lecture Michael for over an hour about how *senpai* should behave toward their *kohai*. Glancing at his watch several times, Michael was not only getting irritated by Ohta's lecture but also starting to resent being talked to in this way.

At a quarter past six, Michael left the office. On his way home, he said to himself, "Why did I have to listen to such nonsense— and on my own time! It's so ridiculous. Who in the world can accept that kind of advice? I don't want this anymore, no matter how much they pay me." Months of accumulated frustration made him decide to leave the company.

The Clash of Cultures in Business

In today's business environment, the mechanics of global business seem to be working on a surface level. We can make quick money transactions by phone or by computer. Consumers can purchase myriad products from different countries. Although trade barriers are still a major topic among politicians, they are slowly but surely decreasing. However, when we look below the surface, we see that global business is in jeopardy because of a newly emerging challenge: the clash of cultures. The more interactions people have with others from different cultural backgrounds, the more challenges arise that are new and complex.

In the Japanese management model, *hito* (people), *mono* (things, fixed assets), and *kane* (money) are the three key resources of business. It is easy to make a money transaction across borders. It is relatively easy to provide products to an overseas market, even with some product modification. But managing *hito* is very different from managing *kane* and *mono*.

Some businesspeople may say, "But we are getting closer and closer to each other. We don't have any cultural problems." Yes, it is possible to transcend cultural differences. That is a premise of this book. However, such statements can be misleading to many businesspeople. As the cross-cultural management researcher, Geert Hofstede, observes:[2]

> When people write about national cultures in the modern world becoming more similar, the evidence cited is usually taken from the level of practices: people dress the same, buy the same products, and use the same fashionable words (symbols); they see the same television shows and movies (heroes); they perform the same sports and leisure activities (rituals). These rather superficial manifestations of culture are sometimes mistaken for all there is; the deeper, underlying level of values, which moreover determine the meaning for people of their practices, is overlooked.

Let us review the first scenario presented in this chapter. As we can see, one mismanaged cross-cultural incident can trigger a crisis in an organization. Jones's comment that the company did not exist for the employees or for the customers but for the shareholders was the last straw for Yamamura and the other Japanese employees. Although Jones had an ethnocentric attitude and was ignorant of Japanese business assumptions (the Japanese have less concern for shareholders and more for employees mainly because the ratio in Japan of individual to institutional shareholders is 30:70, whereas in the United States it is 70:30), the Japanese could not tell if he was playing devil's advocate. They also did not consider the U.S. business environment, which includes strict demands by shareholders and financial-disclosure regulations. The second scenario shows the flip side. Both Michael and Ohta were trying their best, but the gaps in their expectations, assumptions, and perceptions caused their miscommunication. What is needed is a keen insight, not only to see others' expectations, assumptions, and perceptions but also to clarify our own and thus limit the discrepancy between them.

The issues arising from cross-cultural mismanagement are not to be simplified into accusation and blame—although we are often trapped into such responses. Mutual awareness, understanding of different mindsets, and effective cross-cultural communication are essential at an individual level. If organizations want to create this more productive cross-cultural working environment, they have to provide appropriate structural support. In the following chapters I will explain how to provide this support. But first we will examine our cross-cultural environment.

The Mishandling of the Fiftieth Anniversary of Pearl Harbor

The impact of cross-cultural mismanagement is not limited to business organizations. It influences communities, various types of shareholders, political decisions, and eventually the international economy. An unfortunate, yet typical, cross-cultural miscommunication took place between the United States and Japan at the end of 1991, during the fiftieth anniversary of Pearl Harbor.

In 1991 most of the major U.S. and Japanese media were running features about the tragedy of Pearl Harbor and how it had triggered the war between the two countries. Several features also focused on the current "economic war" between the two nations. Despite this negative coverage, some information sources did advocate building collaborative relations between the United States and Japan instead of concentrating on the current friction.[3]

Nowadays, it is difficult to find a U.S. business magazine that does not feature advertisements from Japanese companies. However, under the above circumstances, many Japanese companies decided to withdraw their advertisements from almost all the major

U.S. magazines that featured stories on Pearl Harbor. These companies thought that including advertisements in the magazines would serve to associate "the current Japanese economic intrusion" with the Pearl Harbor attack. Although some Americans might view this reaction as a little extreme, it illustrates two major cultural characteristics of the Japanese: strong conflict avoidance and *jishuku* (self-restraint). Ironically, the decision to withdraw advertisements produced unexpected results. To the great surprise of the Japanese, the American media focused on the millions of lost dollars resulting from the sudden cancellation of the advertisements.[4]

A cross-cultural management study made in 1981 by André Laurent of the European Institute of Business Administration, which shows the different attitudes toward conflict held by the United States and by Japan and other countries, sheds light on the above situation. Laurent questioned over seventeen hundred managers from twelve countries and identified distinct cultural patterns within each country. In one question he asked the managers whether they agreed or disagreed with the following statement: "Most organizations would be better off if conflict could be eliminated forever." Interestingly, only 6 percent of American managers agreed[5] compared with over 80 percent of the Japanese managers. The Japanese have a strong tendency toward conflict avoidance, whereas Americans tend to say, "Something wrong? Let's talk about it."

If the Japanese companies had acknowledged this understanding of American attitudes, they could have gone ahead and printed their advertisements, perhaps with the following text: "In the past, there was a tragic situation between the United States and Japan. In order not to repeat the same mistake, our company is firmly committed to building a strong interdependent relationship with our American partners, employees, customers, and communities. With our five thousand American employees, we will continue to pursue this mission." Such a statement directly addresses the sensitive issues at hand and communicates a positive attitude rather than exhibiting *jishuku* and conflict avoidance. Japanese companies could have transformed a critical situation into an opportunity to improve relationships. Only recently have Japanese companies such as Toyota Motor Corporation and Honda Motor Co. started to proclaim their commitments as well as their accomplishments, primarily through their policies of hiring local American employees and increasing the number of locally manufactured components in their products.

The Clash of Image:
Politicians, Media, and Opinion Leaders

"I want to know about 'Japanese predatorial capitalism' and the motivation behind it." That was the first query from an American manager in one of my seminars. Upon clarification, I found that he was preoccupied by an image of Japan taken primarily from the media. As a supplier to several Japanese manufacturers in the United States, he had experienced frustration and believed in the story of a Japanese economic invasion.

The clash of cultures has two components. First, as mentioned previously, real incidents result from behavioral differences, including organizational decisions and individual comments and actions. The other component is image, and there are many negative images that portray international relationships, especially between the United States and Japan, as "economic war." These images are often created by very real behavioral misunderstandings; however, they are then exaggerated by the media, politicians, and opinion leaders and are transformed into negative stereotypes, which ultimately may influence individual behavior. The American manager in our first scenario was unable to work with his Japanese team because he was bound by such stereotypes.

LEEDS METROPOLITAN UNIVERSITY LEARNING CENTRE

We cannot ignore these negative images, and we must refrain from falling into their trap of ignorance. Politicians who make judgmental and overly generalized comments about another country do not realize that they are showing their own cultural ignorance. When a Japanese politician said, "The quality of American labor is bad," he showed his lack of understanding of U.S. business and lack of experience with American workers. At the same time, an American senator's televised comment that "the Japanese are so unfair that they don't import any foreign cars" revealed that he had never visited Japan. If he had, he would have seen many BMW and Mercedes automobiles. In addition to such blunders by politicians, the media often make cross-cultural situations worse. It has been said, "When a dog bites a man, that is not news. But if a man bites a dog, that is news." The media tends toward sensationalism.

Hiroshi Ando, a former Asahi Press reporter, in his book *Nichibei Jyoho Masatsu* (The Information Friction Between the United States and Japan),[6] clearly shows the inherent problems in journalism, including exaggeration, twisting, and selection of the facts according to a preexisting image. He acknowledges that reporters tended to focus on negative issues and to generalize incidents.

If the politicians and journalists who influence images cultivated minimal cross-cultural skills, we would not see so many image clashes. We should at least keep in mind the following tendencies. First, opinion leaders do not always represent the majority's views. Second, politicians tend to engage in pronationalist rhetoric in order to inflame their electorate. And third, journalism often sensationalizes news events. But by developing our own transcultural competencies, we can avoid the trap of ignorance. In the next chapter we focus on how to manage the clash of cultures in the business environment. First of all, we consider the basic question: "Why culture?"

Chapter Two

Why Culture?

Culture—in all its glory—has taken center stage.
Increased diversity in the American work force, ethnic
strife in Eastern and Central Europe, cultural differences
in cross-border joint ventures, mergers, and acquisitions
are trends that have demonstrated how little many of us
know about cultural differences and how to manage them.
This will be a growth area for the 21st century.
STEPHEN RHINESMITH[1]

Consider whether you agree or disagree with the following statements:

1. "As long as we do business, we speak the same language."
2. "All the Japanese I met in Japan during my business trips spoke good English. So I didn't and won't have any cultural problems."
3. "She isn't new to business. Although this is her first overseas assignment, she will do fine."
4. "We can handle any problems and challenges if we just sit down and discuss things and work together."

The Discounting of Culture

In my years of experience in international business, I have often heard comments such as those above. All are dangerous assumptions in doing business across cultures. The first two statements illustrate the fact that many businesspeople look only at the surface of cultural issues. It is true that some business principles can easily transcend national borders. For example, many businesspeople

13

say that earning money is the bottom line. But it is necessary to clarify the time frame (Will we earn money in the next quarter or next quarter-century?), the priority (Is earning money the ultimate purpose of the organization?), and the process (In what ways do we earn money?). In clarifying such issues, we realize that we cannot ignore cultural differences.

The third statement illustrates another trap. A person who is successful in the domestic environment is not always competent in the international sphere. Likewise, an organization that grows rapidly and successfully at home quite often hits stumbling blocks when trying to enter overseas markets. The fourth statement may appear sound. However, the real issue is the meaning behind the phrase "discuss things and work together." Can we assume that to "discuss" embraces cross-cultural communication skills, including language differences? And what does "work together" mean? How can you confirm that management tools are cross-culturally valid? Can you facilitate a bicultural or multicultural meeting? Without careful consideration, such tasks could be major pitfalls in working across cultures.

In general, businesspeople tend to see culture as something at the opposite end of the spectrum from business. Before entering the field of cross-cultural management, I worked for a decade as a Japanese *sarari-man* ("salary-man") in two big organizations, one Japanese and one American. I was one of those who thought I was too busy to pay any attention to "cultural" matters. Following are some assumptions businesspeople have regarding culture. I admit that I used to hold them too:

- Culture is invisible and intangible. It is therefore not a relevant subject for businesspeople.
- There is no clear definition of culture.
- Culture and business are totally separate issues.

Why has culture been thus discounted? Why do so many people ignore the impact of culture on business? Management scholars often have the same attitude as businesspeople. Nancy Adler, the author of *International Dimensions of Organizational Behavior,* which addresses cross-cultural management issues in the global business context, wrote:[2]

Management professors seem to demonstrate an equivalent culture blindness. A survey of management research published in 24 academic and professional journals over the last decade documented that less than 5 percent of the articles refer to either international or domestic multiculturalism in their research designs or results. American researchers conduct the vast majority of the studies in the United States and yet assume their findings to be universally true. Management researchers, perhaps to an even greater extent than their corporate colleagues, have ignored the influence of culture on organizations.

Perhaps one of the major reasons for discounting culture is the tendency of cultural experts and businesspeople to consider their fields to be mutually exclusive. However, fortunately, during the last two decades many cultural experts have been able to address cultural issues in ways that businesspeople can accept. At the same time, management scholars have also started integrating culture into their business research. Such changes make it possible for us to revise the above assumptions into the following three paradigms:

1. Culture is invisible and intangible. However, culture can be converted into visible and tangible aspects in business management by manifestations of culture.
2. Culture can be systematically defined.
3. Culture and business are seamlessly united. We can see culture in business and business in culture (see Figure 2.1).

What Is Culture?

So, what is culture? Although cultural anthropologists give various definitions, a general definition encompasses the knowledge, language, values, customs, and material objects that are passed from person to person and from generation to generation. Culture includes a sense of self and space, communication and language, dress and appearance, food and feeding habits, time and time consciousness, relationships, values and norms, beliefs and attitudes, mental process and learning, and work habits and practices.[3] In brief, culture might be defined as a person's mental programming, mind software,[4] or mindsets.[5] Given the encompassing nature of

Figure 2.1. The New Business and Culture Paradigm.

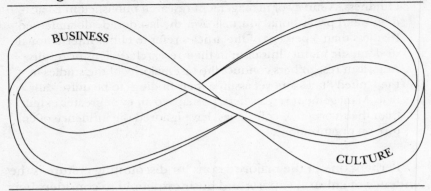

Source: Geonexus Communications, Inc. Copyright © 1994 by Geonexus Communications, Inc. Reproduced by permission.

culture, it is obvious that it influences almost all aspects of management, including organizational factors, such as structure, systems, and strategy; management behaviors and styles, such as leadership, meeting management, and decision making; and functions, such as product development, marketing, and human resources.

Several models have been developed to illustrate culture. Figure 2.2, which shows a modification of the Cummins dual iceberg model,[6] portrays the two cultures of the United States and Japan. The apparent language, behavior, and styles of each culture are the visible parts of the iceberg, while customs, frame of reference, assumed rules, beliefs, and values comprise the deeper, submerged part. Although behaviors are based on the deeper value systems below the water, we tend to respond to other cultures only on a surface level—the tip of the iceberg. In order to truly communicate, we have to explore the frames of reference that exist below sea level.

A key point demonstrated by the iceberg model is that, despite some differences in beliefs and values, cultures often share a common ground. That is why we hear comments such as "Once we got to know that person, we didn't have any more problems." Again, we have to look carefully at such a statement. For some people it is indeed valid, because they do reach and share common ground.

Figure 2.2. The Dual Iceberg Model of Cross-Cultural Relationships.

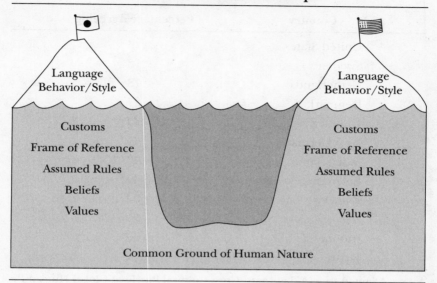

Source: Geonexus Communications, Inc. Copyright © 1994 by Geonexus Communications, Inc. Reproduced by permission.

Such elements as trust, sincerity, and integrity are vital for building any successful business relationships regardless of cultural differences. However, in business, we see many areas of difference that sometimes cause people to forget that a common ground does exist. For instance, research by André Laurent demonstrates the impact of national culture on management practices (Table 2.1). He asked managers from different countries whether they agree with the following: "It is important for a manager to have at hand precise answers to most of the questions that his subordinates may raise about their work."[7]

The results indicated that managers from different national cultures had different assumptions, expectations, and perceptions of what management should be. Although 77 percent of Japanese managers agreed with the statement, only 13 percent of U.S. managers agreed. Clearly, it is critical to look at differences carefully before assuming a common ground.

**Table 2.1. The Impact of
National Culture on Management Practice.**

Country	Percentage Agreeing
United States	13
Sweden	13
Netherlands	18
Denmark	27
United Kingdom	30
West Germany	40
Switzerland	40
Belgium	49
France	59
Italy	59
Indonesia	67
Japan	77

Source: Adapted from A. Laurent, "Cross-Cultural Puzzle of Global Human Re-source Management," *Human Resource Management, 25*(1), Spring 1986.

Cultural Problem or Management Problem?

I often hear the following comment from clients: "Our problems here are not cultural. Rather, they are about management issues." This comment contains the assumption that cultural problems are different from management problems. In order to respond, I would like to share the following two situations.

In a Japanese company operating in the United States, a newly assigned manager from Japan spoke at his first meeting with American employees and emphasized that, as far as possible, he would like to continue the same policies and systems as his predecessor. The reaction from the American staff members was "If he doesn't have any ideas of his own, why did the company assign him here? He doesn't seem to have any initiative!"

In an American company operating in Japan, a newly assigned manager from the United States spoke at his first meeting with his

Japanese employees and emphasized that he would like to change the current systems because he was assigned as a change agent and change meant progress. The reaction from the Japanese staff members was "He doesn't know our situation in Japan. How can he bring about change?"

Although their behaviors were different, both of these managers shared a common mistake: they did not acknowledge the local culture or build an initial trust with their subordinates. Both were too focused on getting good reviews on their assignments from headquarters and paid more attention to the requirements of headquarters than to the local operations. Such mistakes are typical in companies that are going global. In both cases the local staff will say, "This person is always looking out for what headquarters thinks, not for how we feel!" This is a structural management issue and presents one of the most difficult challenges for an organization in the process of going global. These managers lost their credibility in the eyes of the local staff because of differences in expectations regarding leadership behavior, which is a cross-cultural communication problem.

Ultimately, it is not a question of whether the problem is cultural or managerial. What is needed is a holistic view and a nonlinear way of thinking in order to perceive the cultural implications of management issues and to handle both individual behavioral issues and corporate structural issues.

Are We Portraying Other Cultures Accurately or Inaccurately?

Another common mistake we often make when handling cross-cultural issues is to confuse stereotypes with descriptions of national cultures. Stereotypes are subjective and preconceived notions, generally about people from other cultures, whereas descriptions of national cultures are based on statistically tested societal norms and often appear in and arise from cross-cultural research data.

Stereotypes are quite often judgmental, evaluative, and negative. When I was working for an American company in Tokyo, I frequently heard my Japanese colleagues and managers stereotyping the U.S. home office staff in the following way:

"They work only from nine to five."

"They don't have any loyalty to the company."

"They don't cooperate with each other."

On the other hand, I often hear the following stereotypes from Americans regarding Japanese businesspeople:

"They are secretive."

"They all dress the same."

"They are not logical."

Many movies and publications featuring Japan tend to include some samurai image or illustration, thus fostering another stereotype: that all Japanese are martial artists. In truth, the Japanese population of martial arts practitioners is much less than the populations of tennis or golf players. Stereotypes often overgeneralize, and in many cases they express a negative attitude toward others.

On the other hand, descriptions of national cultures are not evaluative. They accurately describe the norm for the group to which the person belongs rather than the characteristics of a specific individual. Some of them appear in statistically and scientifically valid cross-cultural research data (discussed in Chapter Seven). In citing descriptions of national cultures, however, we have to remember the meaning of what John Condon, a trailblazer in the field of intercultural communication, observed: "All variations may exist in any one society."[8] It is said that the United States is an individualistic society while Japan is a group-oriented society. But, of course, there are some individualistic Japanese and some group-oriented Americans. We say, "That's common sense," but we often forget this common sense.

Portraying other cultures is not easy. In fact, it is one of the major challenges for cross-cultural trainers and consultants. In general, cultural experts tend to emphasize the differences between people rather than the similarities, while businesspeople, economists, and many management scholars tend to discount cultural differences. It is important to clarify and present both similarities *and* differences.

"Culture" in Japan

Despite all the revered traditions and the indigenous arts, such as flower arrangement, tea ceremonies, and martial arts, the broader concept of culture, which includes the norms and value systems of a group of people, has not taken root in Japan. There are two main reasons for this:

1. Many people concerned with cultural activities reinforce the narrow definition of culture by emphasizing specific arts (for example, tea ceremonies and Kabuki). Given this narrow definition, the broader meaning of culture cannot become established.
2. Because of negative connotations associated with the view that "Japan is so unique that Westerners cannot share the same socioeconomic system," many Japanese media tend to avoid discussion of cultural issues in international political and economic talks. They think that talking about culture may justify such a viewpoint. This dynamic is especially prevalent when friction over the U.S.–Japan trade imbalance is being discussed.

As a result, many Japanese media commentators and scholars avoid the assumption that culture has anything to do with management or political-economic activities. They tend to believe that debating cultural issues only leads to a dead end where they can make no progress and to make comments such as: "Because this is deeply related to cultural differences, we cannot really do anything." It is difficult for Japanese media to handle these differences synergistically. Until recently, few systematic and constructive approaches toward culture have appeared in Japanese written analysis. Consequently, the Japanese tend to overreact when confronted by cultural debate. For instance, Samuel Huntington's 1993 article, "The Clash of Civilizations?" in which he addressed the cultural concerns that Japanese have kept hidden away, shook the Japanese media.[9] For more than a year, the article was featured in various newspapers and magazines, and Huntington was invited to Japan to take part in open forums. Given this lack of a broader concept of culture in Japan, it may be difficult to engage in open dialogue of cross-cultural issues.

Cross-Cultural Impediments for U.S. Management Experts

Despite the current fad for cultural issues, including organizational culture and cultural diversity, much of the current literature does not place organizations in a global, multicultural context. A great deal has been written comparing the U.S. management system with the Japanese one, but it is difficult to find such work with a systematic cross-cultural perspective. If a researcher is not aware of his or her own cultural filters, the observations will be valid only within the researcher's culture. Some descriptions of Japanese management written by U.S. management experts demonstrate this cross-cultural impediment.

For instance, in a 1993 article in the *Harvard Business Review,* Tracy Goss, Richard Pascale, and Anthony Athos admired Honda's *waigaya* sessions (*waigaya* comes from *waiwai gayagaya,* which describes a situation of informal and noisy chattering). They said, "At Honda, any employee, however junior, can call for a *waigaya* session. The rules are that people lay their cards on the table and speak directly about problems."[10] Within six months, a Japanese monthly magazine, *Sentaku,*[11] which is also read by Japanese business executives, featured an article titled "Collapse of Soichiro-ism" (referring to Soichiro Honda, the founder of Honda). It quoted the current CEO of Honda as refuting *waigaya.* The article also pointed out, as did other published Japanese comments, that Honda is losing the uniqueness of its original corporate culture and becoming a big company just like Toyota or Nissan.

This discrepancy in observations about *waigaya* and the transition of Honda's corporate culture is not just the result of the time lag between Japan and the United States. It is true that Honda is well known for its *waigaya* and other peculiar Honda traditions. In fact, some Japanese employees who joined Honda from other Japanese automotive companies were surprised by the openness of Honda's corporate culture. However, American employees may read about the *waigaya* system and take it out of context, thinking, "That's great. I can speak out regardless of my experience and age." If they do, they will probably hit a wall of resistance from their Japanese *senpai* (senior member) and learn a hard lesson. Those who have working experience in Japanese organizations can tell just how open a *waigaya* session really is. It does not mean that a recent college graduate can call a meeting freely. As a friend who works for a Japanese company that is highly regarded by U.S. management experts told me, "Some American applicants have an overly idealized view of our company. Then they realize it is still a Japanese company and they get disappointed." Such companies may not be as rigid as other, more traditional, Japanese companies, but they are not as flexible as Americans may wish.

Another way that U.S. management experts reveal their cultural filters is in their belief in a strong organizational hero. Geert Hofstede points this out:[12]

> U.S. management literature rarely distinguishes between the values of founders and significant leaders, and the value of the bulk of the organization's members. Descriptions of organizational cultures are often only based on statements by corporate heroes. . . . Organizations can look very different from the top than from the middle or bottom where the actual work is done.

It is especially difficult for outsiders to see through the *tatemae* (surface) of Japanese organizations to the *honne* (de facto) basis upon which they really function. If they do not have the contextual literacy to read between the lines of the annual report or other corporate documents, questionnaires, and surveys, then they, as well as Japanese scholars, can easily dismiss critical *honne* organizational dynamics. It is true that outside researchers can sometimes provide new perspectives that insiders cannot see. However, it is surprising that there are so many overly idealized articles about Japanese management.

Several non–U.S. scholars have also pointed out the cross-cultural impediment of U.S. management experts. Nancy Adler and Mariann Jelinek wrote:[13]

> Americans' rejections of most types of determinism may also explain in part why the burgeoning popularity of the organization culture concept has not, as yet, integrated with a commensurate interest in cross-cultural approaches to management. Perhaps it is not surprising that much of the most significant cross-cultural management research has been conducted by non–U.S. based scholars.

This fact leads us to a critical drawback of managing organizational culture. An American strategic consultant working with Japanese companies said, "I don't care about cultural differences between the United States and Japan, because I worked with many companies in the United States. They have different corporate cultures and we are experienced in analyzing the differences between these companies." This comment illustrates not only the cross-cultural impediments to seeing national cultural issues but also the confusion between organizational culture (within a company) and national culture (within a country).

Although there is no consensus among scholars about the difference between national culture and organizational culture, the key question is in the focus. According to Hofstede, "At the national level cultural differences reside mostly in values, less in practices. At the organizational level, cultural differences reside mostly in practices, less in values."[14] Per-Olof Berg stated, "If a company, for example, moves from a national to an international context, the national-cultural character of the company (which previously was completely neglected) will be of the utmost importance."[15] If we focus on business practices, such as the degree of control of employees, we see more differences on a corporate basis. These are relatively easy to observe. However, in order to focus on the national cultural influence, we have to infer and then highlight the underlying assumptions that are unconscious and taken for granted.[16]

When I joined an American International Group (AIG) operation in Japan after working for Toshiba, I was able to observe different business practices clearly. Although most of the employees of AIG in Tokyo were Japanese, there were significant differences from Toshiba. The decision cycle was much faster than in Toshiba and the Japanese employees' dress code was much more casual. However, whenever we had meetings with other U.S. expatriates or visitors from headquarters, the behavior of the Japanese employees, by contrast, reminded me that they, and I, were Japanese. Through such cross-cultural encounters, submerged assumptions came to the surface. For instance, distinctly different communication styles were evident: the Japanese style was indirect and used a kind of spiral logic, while the U.S. style was direct and used a cut-to-the-chase approach. The Japanese employees often paused silently for long periods of time, which frustrated their American counterparts. We have to be careful in handling organizational culture and national culture and in discerning their implications. Otherwise, either or both of the cultures could act as blind spots.

In terms of understanding and awareness of organizational culture and national culture, Japan is even further behind than the United States, because the concept of culture in behavioral science is not well established in Japan. Charles Hampden-Turner put it best:[17]

> Perhaps the Japanese exaggerate the incomparable nature of a culture isolated for centuries from the rest of the world, but perhaps Americans exaggerate the value of their own psychological yardsticks in taking the measure of foreigners.

Both American and Japanese managers need to realize the cross-cultural impediments that limit their perception and hinder them from working effectively across cultures in the global arena. The next chapter explains the first step in improving cross-cultural situations—an effective use of the language that is most commonly spoken in today's global business: English.

Chapter Three

Language Matters

Do not worry about people not knowing you.
Worry more about not knowing other people.
CONFUCIAN ANALECTS 1:16[1]

It is becoming easier for native English speakers to communicate across cultures as more people start speaking English in the global business community. And as just about everyone who is linked by the Internet is communicating in English, it seems that we have transcended language barriers. However, language barriers still exist, even in this emerging English-speaking environment. The less awareness of language issues we have, the greater the possibility that miscommunications may occur. One critical view that is often missing is how nonnative English speakers learn English and how they feel when communicating in English. By developing such awareness, we can maximize the benefit of English as a major global business communication tool.

In this chapter, I would like to cover cross-cultural language issues by offering some insights for English speakers as a nonnative English speaker. To do this, I will focus on the U.S.–Japan situation to demonstrate the distinct language and cultural differences between the two countries.

Note: In this chapter, I would like to acknowledge John Kent and Wendy Fitzgerald for their advice.

Different Assumptions:
The Japanese and the Americans

Successful global communication requires the recognition of several central cross-cultural issues:

- Realizing the link between language, cultural values, and business behaviors
- Casting off false assumptions and an overreliance on spoken-language ability, for example, "If I can speak the language, I won't have any cultural problems" or "All bilingual people are biculturally competent in business"
- Understanding the different levels of language infrastructure in the United States and in other countries, for example, the accessibility of English in Japan and of Japanese in the United States

The Japanese and the Americans have almost opposite assumptions regarding their own language. If you are not Japanese and speak some Japanese, you will often receive compliments from the Japanese. For example, if you say, *"Hajimemashite, dozo yoroshiku onegaishimasu"* ("How do you do? Good to see you"), a Japanese may say to you, "Wow! Your Japanese is really great. Where did you learn to speak so well?" On the other hand, in the United States noncitizens rarely receive such compliments about their English. While many Japanese believe that only the Japanese can learn Japanese and that *gaijin* (foreigners) can never master their language, many Americans believe that everyone should be able to speak English. This assumption gap often causes communication problems. Thus, we have to think not only about the obvious barriers posed by language differences but also about these indirect barriers caused by lack of awareness and assumption gaps.

How the Japanese Study English

We begin with the following scenario.

Mr. Hammer is the director of international marketing at a large American multinational company. He is in Tokyo visiting the company's Japan branch office and giving a presentation to a group of senior managers at the Japanese operation. All twelve managers are Japanese. Twenty minutes into the presentation, Mr. Hammer has not had a single question from any of the Japanese managers. By this time, he is becoming uncomfortable with the stony silence and is trying to figure out the managers' level of understanding. Since he enjoys foreign languages, he had bought a Japanese phrase book and studied a little on the plane from the United States. One phrase he remembers is *"Wakarimasuka,"* which translates as "Do you understand?" To see if the Japanese managers understand his presentation, he suddenly asks, *"Wakarimasuka?"* No response, so he repeats his question in English: "Do you understand?" No response but dead silence. The managers look upset: their faces reflect a disgruntled, stony resentment.

If you do not understand why the Japanese managers were upset, the following will provide a clear insight. In most cases, English is used more than Japanese in U.S.–Japan cross-cultural situations. However, there are many pitfalls when speaking English to Japanese, and by understanding how the Japanese study English, you may become aware of potential problems and how to improve communication.

In junior high school, the Japanese spend four to six class hours per week for three years studying English. Students in high school spend six to eight class hours per week for another three years studying English. In Japan, 95 percent of junior high school graduates go directly on to high school and the high school dropout rate is 2 percent, so 93.1 percent of Japanese spend at least one thousand hours learning English. In addition, English can be seen everywhere in Japan, from neon signs to the English slogans printed on T-shirts.

Although so many hours are spent learning English and the visibility of English is so pervasive in the environment, the Japanese are not good speakers of English. In a survey of the average test scores of the Test of English as a Foreign Language exam between 1994 and 1995, *Japan ranked the fourth lowest of twenty-seven Asian countries.* Countries such as Singapore, India, and the Philippines ranked higher. The only four countries that scored lower than Japan were Thailand, South Korea, Bangladesh, and Yemen. In terms of English comprehension, the average level for Japanese businesspeople is 0+ to 1 on a scale of 0 to 5 on the Language Proficiency Interview, another test of competency in English. Most Japanese seldom use English as a communication tool. Ironically, most Japanese high school teachers of English are not able to speak English!

Why are the Japanese so bad at learning English? There are several reasons. First, from the linguistic point of view, Japanese has a very different sentence structure from English and other European languages. Chinese is more similar to English in terms of the order of words in a sentence. Second, Japanese has fewer than two hundred different vowel and consonant sounds, while English has about two thousand. This means that the hearing range of Japanese is one-tenth that of native English speakers. The third reason is psychological. Although the Japanese study English for over a thousand hours, the main purpose is to pass the notorious college entrance examinations. They learn by memorizing obsolete idioms like "It rains cats and dogs" and analyzing grammar, which is not useful for real communication.

Besides this fever to learn English in order to pass the college entrance examinations, many Japanese have ambivalent feelings toward English. They may have a strong inferiority complex about speaking English, having studied for so many hours but still being unable to communicate well. This sense of inferiority may result in a fragile sense of pride. In addition, some Japanese who had to learn English for entrance examinations and/or business purposes have a sense of failure when it comes to speaking. These mixed feelings and emotions about speaking English often cause subtle, yet crucial, cross-cultural problems.

Pitfalls in Speaking English to the Japanese

Given the above assumptions and difficulties concerning language, it is possible to offend the Japanese without realizing it, as did Mr. Hammer with the phrase *"Wakarimasuka."* Following are some basic guidelines for businesspeople on ways to avoid pitfalls in speaking English to the Japanese. For instance, the following comments are often misinterpreted by the Japanese:

"Why?"

"Do you understand?"

"Say it again."

The question "Why?" is too direct, and the Japanese may take it to mean that you are challenging them. In Japanese business conversation, "Why" is seldom used, except when a client is speaking to a vendor. (The customer is like God in Japan, and God can ask, "Why.") One American manager who was working with a Japanese subsidiary said to me, "Please tell the Japanese managers that it is not our intention to be rude or offensive by asking why. That's how we are trained." Older Japanese especially believe that asking why is rude. Again, each nationality needs to understand the other's intention. It is possible to ask why without saying, "Why?" One useful technique is reflective listening, also called the "mirror technique" by psychiatrists and counselors (see Exhibit 3.1). By

---

Exhibit 3.1. Reflective Listening.

Reflective listening offers techniques for asking why without using the word "Why?" When using reflective listening, we repeat the other person's words. For instance:

"How did the meeting go?"

"We had a heavy discussion."

"A heavy discussion?"

"Yeah, Nakamura-san started playing hardball."

"Nakamura-san?"

"You know. All he is concerned about is money."

"Money? Oh, budget problem."

In order to make reflective listening work, empathy and patience are important. It is effective when talking about sensitive issues. In addition, this technique is beneficial in cross-cultural situations; you can avoid using words that the other person does not know by repeating what he or she has already said.

---

repeating key words in another person's statements, it is possible to further the conversation, thus gaining more detailed information.

"Do you understand?" also is too direct. Japanese schoolteachers and customers may use this question because they are in a higher position than their students or the vendors. If you say, "Do you understand?" in English, the Japanese may be intimidated and feel that their English really is poor. If you say it in Japanese, *"Wakarimasuka,"* it sounds even more condescending. One good technique is to take the blame for poor communication on your own shoulders by saying, "Am I clear?" or "Is it okay?" (Both may be translated in Japanese as *"Yoroshii deshouka."*) Such phrases help to clarify information without offending anyone. One problem is that many teachers of Japanese language to English speakers do not deal with such subtle but critical issues, and they go ahead and teach the students to say *"Wakarimasuka,"* thus causing the communication problem Mr. Hammer encountered.

The Japanese may interpret the phrase "Say it again" as "Your English is terrible. Correct your poor pronunciation." Applying the same logic as in "Do you understand?" it is better to ask for repetition by saying, "I'm sorry. I didn't hear."

Also keep the following in mind:

- Japanese are better readers of English, whereas their oral comprehension is more limited.
- Japanese can usually understand more when you modify your English by using unambiguous and consistent words.
- Be sensitive to differences in communication styles: for instance, the Japanese language contains more formality and indirectness than English.

From American English to International English

The above techniques will help you not only to avoid language pitfalls but also to maximize your English communication potential, especially if you are also able to modify your language into a so-called international English. Nonnative English-speaking people are the native speakers of international English, the most commonly spoken language in the global business community. Considering the more than one thousand hours that Japanese spend learning English, it behooves Americans to become familiar with international English in order to improve communication and mutual understanding. Using international English is one of the core skills for global managers. Many programs and articles give advice on how to speak a form of international English with nonnative speakers. Following are the key points for communicating in international English:

1. Check your words per minute (wpm). It is estimated that the average speed of conversational English is from 125 to 150 wpm. Rapid speakers easily talk at a rate of over 180 wpm. However, the majority of Japanese cannot understand more than 120 wpm.
2. Become comfortable with silence. Consider that silence can contain much meaning. Do not interrupt Japanese while they are being quiet.
3. Simplify sentence structure:
   • Limit yourself to one idea per sentence.
   • Try to use no more than fifteen words per sentence.
   • Use time words such as *first, second,* or *last* to separate ideas or parts of longer descriptions.
   • Avoid tag questions after an explanation or description (for example, "You didn't go, did you?").
   • Avoid negative contractions, such as *can't* or *shouldn't.*
   • Avoid questions that contain several *or*'s.
   • Avoid reductions, such as *gonna, didja,* or *wouldja.*
4. Be clear:
   • Avoid slang (for example, "That's really bad" or "That's really cool").
   • Avoid words that have more than two meanings (for example, "That's *outrageous*").
   • Make sure your pronunciation is correct.
   • Enunciate clearly.
   • Avoid idioms (for example, "I'm tied up all day").
   • Avoid culturally specific jokes and expressions (for example, those that relate to sports, television shows, or games).

These points probably seem like common sense, but they can be difficult to put into practice. I have observed many cross-cultural meetings and negotiations and have found that only a very few people actually use international English. It is crucial for both the Japanese and Americans to learn how to work in a multilingual environment; otherwise conversations may result in the following type of exchange:

Japanese: "Please speak clearly and slowly."
American: "You bet!"
Japanese: "Bet? How much?"
American: "Oh boy!"
Japanese: "Excuse me. I'm becoming forty-five this year."
American: "Hey! You've got me!"
Japanese: "I gata what?"

Part Two

Transcultural Management for Individuals and Organizations

Chapter Four

Globalization and Cultural Intervention

Culture is the most subtle aspect of organization, but it can play a formidable role in helping or hindering a global strategy.
GEORGE S. YIP[1]

The preceding chapters have addressed the initial cultural issues—avoiding cultural ignorance and stereotypes and enhancing language and communication skills—that must be addressed when striving for transcultural competency. In this chapter we turn to the global organization and address the stages of globalization that are common to many companies. We also examine how cultural interventions can help to produce effective global geocentric organizations.

Stages of Globalization

Although scholars differ in the terms, definitions, and interpretations they use to describe global companies, most advocates of globalization would probably agree with the types of global organization shown in Figure 4.1.[2] This model illustrates the stages, or evolution, of global corporations in terms of cultural perspectives and organizational type.

In order to measure the degree of globalization within a company, we have to focus on the cultural perspectives and attitudes in the organization. This focus is crucial because (1) no single criterion

37

Figure 4.1. Stages of Globalization.

Phase	Type of Company	Cultural Perspective
I:	International	Ethnocentric
II:	Multinational	Polycentric
III:	Multiregional	Regiocentric
IV:	Global	Geocentric

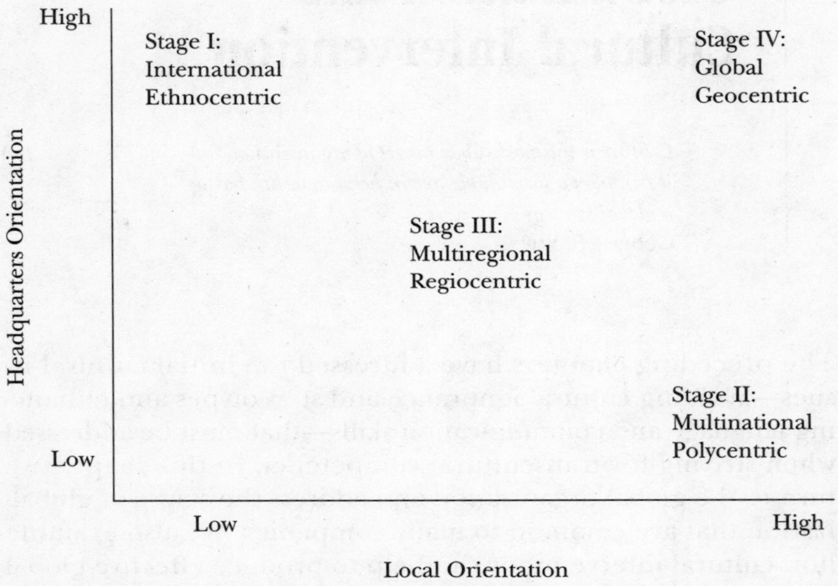

High

Stage I:
International
Ethnocentric

Stage IV:
Global
Geocentric

Headquarters Orientation

Stage III:
Multiregional
Regiocentric

Stage II:
Multinational
Polycentric

Low

Low

High

Local Orientation

of globalization, such as ownership or the number of nationals overseas, is sufficient and (2) external and quantifiable measures, such as the percentage of investment overseas or the distribution of equity by nationality, are useful but not enough.[3] Changing systems and structures from a domestic operation to a world headquarters or introducing a global matrix structure alone does not necessarily make a company truly global.

The first stage of globalization is the *international ethnocentric* corporation. This type of company is headquarters-oriented. Its corporate belief is that "we, the home country nationals, are superior to, more trustworthy, and more reliable than any foreigners in headquarters or the subsidiaries."[4] All key management positions are centered in the domestic headquarters. Home country nationals are recruited and trained for all international positions.[5] In this stage, expatriates are in the teacher mode: teaching "our methods to them" is the general attitude. As a result, they have great difficulty communicating in different languages and accepting cultural differences.[6]

The second stage is the *multinational polycentric* corporation. After learning a hard lesson in the first ethnocentric stage and realizing that local needs exist, most companies shift their approach and "go to the other extreme by assuming that local people always know what is best for them."[7] They assign host country nationals to the key positions in local subsidiaries. As a result, the local orientation is high, and the number of expatriates tends to drop compared to the number in international ethnocentric companies. The role of expatriates is to exert minimum control and to report to headquarters. When an ethnocentric corporation changes to a polycentric organization, some people at headquarters may think they are losing control over local subsidiaries.

The third stage is the *multiregional "regiocentric"* corporation. The regiocentric message is: "Regional insiders know what neighboring countries want."[8] Regiocentrism tries to integrate international ethnocentric organizations with multinational polycentric operations by giving autonomy and management responsibilities to regional headquarters. However, because of the lack of global integration, intraregional conflict over resource allocation, and differing interests, in most cases regiocentrism compromises ethnocentrism and polycentrism rather than transcending the two. Expatriates from headquarters have to cover several countries within the region. That is a challenging mission unless they have regional cultural and business expertise. Personnel exchange also occurs not across the region but within the region, which may limit interregional communications and global career paths for regional managers.

The *global geocentric* corporation represents the final stage and direction of global organizations. It requires collaboration between subsidiaries and headquarters in order to establish universal standards and permissible local variations, on the basis of which key decisions are made.[9] Geocentrism, although costly in terms of communication, travel expenses, and time, pursues the performance of the total enterprise more objectively. Worldwide use of resources is made possible by transcending the first three stages.[10] In this stage, the cross-cultural interaction becomes more complex and important; the geocentric system is highly interdependent and more people have the opportunity to experience working across borders. They come not only from headquarters but also from each local office, because they are linked into an integrated network of operations designed to achieve the multidimensional strategic objectives of efficiency, responsiveness, and innovation.[11]

Stumbling Blocks to Globalization

When we compare the pros and cons of these four stages (Table 4.1), it becomes clear why it is so difficult to reach the global geocentric stage and why many companies return to the first stage, international ethnocentrism, while keeping a multinational polycentric corporate appearance. Many headquarters employees cannot bear the arduous work involved as cross-cultural interactions increase. Because of the daily frustration of working with local subsidiaries, they are caught in the shortsighted temptation to cut expenses and revert to relentless ethnocentrism before they can achieve and harvest the real fruits of globalization.

Major companies in the United States and Japan are striving to become truly global organizations. However, as Howard Perlmutter, the advocate of the geocentric model, stated in 1969, "The route to pervasive geocentric thinking is long and tortuous."[12] Not many corporations have actually reached a global geocentric stage, mainly because of the power dynamics between the headquarters operation, which tends toward ethnocentrism, and the local operation, which often strongly insists on becoming polycentric without accepting the worldwide concept of the company.

Perlmutter listed the obstacles to geocentrism by categorizing both the external environmental and internal intraorganizational aspects. Interestingly enough, some of these external factors, such as military secrecy associated with research in the home country or distrust caused by the lack of an efficient international monetary

Table 4.1. Pros and Cons of Globalization.

Stage	Pros	Cons
I: International ethnocentric	Strong integration Cost efficiency for the short term	Lack of good feedback from local operation Slow to fully adapt local designs, manufacture in other countries, or make other major investments
II: Multinational polycentric	Fulfills all service needs (products, manufacturing, and R&D) Fosters a sense of autonomy among local employees	Waste from duplication of effort Inefficient use of local expertise on a global scale
III: Multiregional regiocentric	Regional integration of resources Closer market and customer interface than Stage I	Greater assumption of homogeneity in regions than actual diversity Lack of expertise sharing on an interregional basis
IV: Global geocentric	Worldwide use of resources Worldwide learning and sharing Greater commitment to a worldwide goal Multicultural synergy	High cost of communication, traveling Time spent in decision-making process Education about global objectives Potential multicultural conflict

Source: Adapted from S. H. Robock and K. Simmonds, *International Business and Multinational Enterprises,* 4th ed. (Burr Ridge, Ill.: Irwin, 1989), pp. 219–220.

system, have been declining during the last two decades. Instead, most of the internal factors, such as mutual distrust between the home country staff and foreign executives or linguistic and other communication difficulties of a cultural nature, have remained the same or even increased with the more frequent cross-cultural interactions required between headquarters and the local branches. The rise of internal concerns makes it difficult and complex for headquarters and local branches to collaborate. The key to real globalization for a company is the ability to manage and transform this tug-of-war between headquarters and local branches into a positive strategic dialogue rather than to allow it to become a "blame-the-others" game. Thus, along with the evolution of globalization, the role of cultural interventions has become more critical than ever.

Types of Cultural Intervention

As corporations have evolved into more geocentric organizations, *cultural interventions* (planned organization-wide programs that focus on cultural issues) have also shifted their focus and expanded their domain. Initial cultural interventions for business communities included predeparture training for the expatriate assignee, with cultural orientation regarding the sociohistory and religion of the foreign country (country orientation), language training, survival information, and help with psychological adjustment to prevent culture shock.

The Peace Corps is one originator of such predeparture training. In 1965 the Peace Corps used fifty-eight universities and several nonacademic organizations as training centers.[13] The fact that institutionalized predeparture training started in the 1960s and spread during the 1970s coincides with the evolution of the globalization process. During those decades, major companies were still at the international ethnocentric stage and were sending expatriates to local subsidiaries; general awareness about cross-cultural training was relatively low. Since then the need for predeparture training programs has become clearer to many major corporations. According to a 1979 survey of eighty multinational companies, 32 percent of the respondents had formal predeparture training.[14] It is estimated that in 1992 nearly half of all major companies were providing some kind of cross-cultural training.[15]

As major corporations moved to the multinational polycentric and multiregional regiocentric stages during the 1980s, different types of cross-cultural training programs evolved. Host country workforce training for those who work with expatriates is one type of program. For instance, in a Japanese subsidiary of a U.S. multinational company, the Japanese employees may learn how to work with American expatriates. Another program includes training for nonexpatriates who are frequent travelers or who work with overseas operations at headquarters.

Now that global companies (and companies that are striving to become global organizations) require more communication and personnel exchange overseas, new types of training and consulting programs are being demanded. Headquarters not only sends expatriates abroad but also receives "inpatriates" from overseas operations. These inpatriates are foreign engineers, middle managers, and senior managers with two- to three-year assignments at headquarters. More staff members are involved in cross-cultural interactions through E-mail, teleconferencing, and videoconferencing. Each business function (marketing, human resources, finance, and so on) holds a quarterly or semiannual international conference that includes employees from various countries. It becomes clear that multicultural team development is needed at headquarters as well as at each local office.

In addition to these intraorganizational cross-cultural interactions, corporations have increased their external interactions with overseas customers, vendors, and strategic partners. Consequently, the cross-cultural training and consulting field has expanded from predeparture training programs, which originally focused on individual adjustment and cultural awareness, to strategic interventions that deal with core management concerns, such as developing multicultural work teams, aligning cross-cultural strategic alliances, and facilitating the business-planning process in a cross-cultural environment. Such changes do not mean that predeparture training is losing its value. Although many companies still cannot see the real benefit of such training, the need is increasing due to newly emerging markets, such as China and the Eastern European countries. However, the focus of programs may have to expand from imparting traditional cultural information to addressing contemporary issues, from individual behavioral differences to strategic organization concerns, and from general business issues to industry-specific issues.

For example, ten or twenty years ago, imparting culture-specific information concerning business card etiquette was very valuable. Indeed, American businesspeople sometimes make critical mistakes when exchanging business cards, so this topic is still often covered in training programs. However, it is not a core topic for cross-cultural training in the 1990s and beyond. The *Wall Street Journal* addressed this transition by introducing the concept of multicultural management seminars:[16]

> These seminars [multicultural management], which began to pop up in Europe in the 1980s, go beyond the traditional short course on how an expatriate executive can cope with the folkways of a particular country or region. The goal is to help executives (expatriate or not) come to terms with a wide range of problem solving. The trainers try to change attitudes and challenge biases—rather than merely parroting a list of admonitions against, say, patting a Thai child on the head or arriving late for a meeting in Frankfurt.

Furthermore, Sharon Richards, intercultural training manager for Intel Corporation, offers guidelines for trainer selection and development:[17]

> The criteria should not only be that they are from that country and know the language and culture, but they should also be versed in current business practices. They must be able to apply intercultural theory and training to business situations, needs, and applications. Corporate intercultural training must go beyond the surface culture of food, dress, and language to provide the deeper understanding of individual awareness—how we operate and communicate from our own culture—and how all cultures can best work together.

The Expanding Domain of Cross-Cultural Trainers and Consultants

As mentioned above, cross-cultural training and consulting began with such critical issues as cultural adjustment, counseling, country orientation, and relocation support, which have high cultural implications in nonbusiness living (labeled "Area I" in Figure 4.2). Cross-cultural training and consulting activities are now beginning to focus more on issues of management, human resources, and marketing, which not only have high cultural implications (soft issues) but also have high business implications (hard issues). The more technical issues of business—accounting, finance, and information systems, which comprise Area III—have low cultural implications but high business implications. Area II demands more integrated hard (business) and soft (culture) skill sets than Areas I and III. While much has been written about Area I, not many works have focused on Area II, despite the increasing demands of more and more companies that are striving for globalization. Noel M. Tichy has advocated a new framework for global development, "compressed action learning," which blends management development with organization development.[18] It is unfortunate that

Figure 4.2. Areas of Cross-Cultural Training and Consulting.

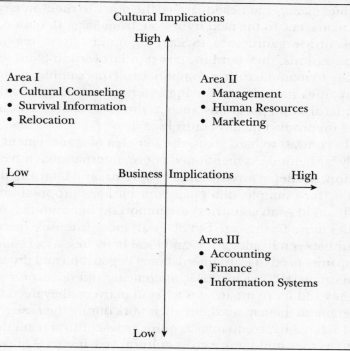

"hard" management consultants and "soft" organization development specialists rarely work together. What we need is to blend the two, based on a cross-cultural perspective.

Globalization requires bridging the gap between hard and soft. (See Figure 4.3.) In hard management areas, such as strategy, information systems, and production, actions that are listed as examples of achieving global evolution are more easily identified than in soft management areas such as human resources management and organization development. When companies plan to go abroad, they need to do market research and to learn export tactics and legal and logistic issues. After they build overseas branches and move from Stage I, international ethnocentric organizations, to Stage II, multinational polycentric organizations, they promote host country–driven marketing by realizing local needs and also begin product modification. At the same time, in order to coordinate other national branches, they often introduce a matrix structure into their organizations, in which overseas managers have two allegiances and lines of reporting: one to their special-function or product manager at headquarters, the other to their overseas general managers. In the next transition, from Stage II, multinational polycentric organizations, to Stage III, multiregional regiocentric organizations, they tend to start standardization from product quality to manufacturing components. For example, quite a few companies started introducing International Organization for Standardization programs, such as the ISO9000 series, which focuses on product quality-control systems.

In contrast to hard areas, the soft area of management is relatively far behind. As mentioned above, international travel information, predeparture training programs, and learning dos and don'ts (for example, don't pass your business proposal with your left hand in Arab countries) are important but minimal. As companies move from Stage I to Stage II, more intensive discussions occur between headquarters and local branches. As a result, these companies need to learn international negotiation and distant communication skills, such as teleconferencing and videoconferencing. As they add more inpatriates to headquarters, they need to offer programs to them to maximize their work during their assignments.

In Stage III, companies require cross-cultural team development as they build more cross-cultural task forces. At this point,

Figure 4.3. Global Evolution: Bridging the Gap Between "Hard" and "Soft."

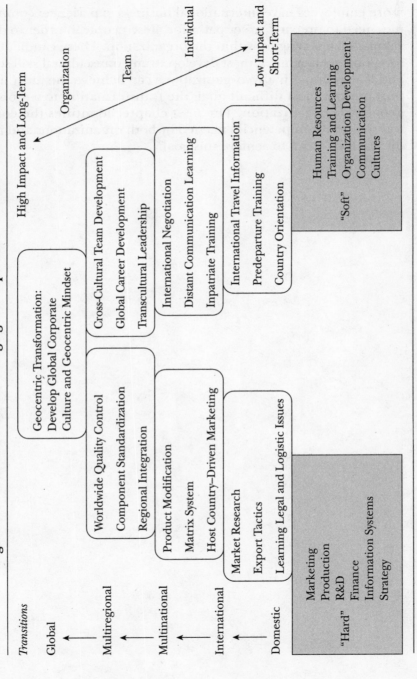

more employees have international business experience; companies need to prepare career paths for these people in order to develop global managers within the organization. These candidates for global management must develop strong transcultural skill sets and leadership. Finally, organizations can achieve the most important, but most difficult goal: the transformation to a global geocentric organization. The next chapter identifies the core transcultural competencies needed by both organizations and individuals in order to achieve this goal.

Chapter Five

Enabling Global Organizations
Five Core Competencies

Research on multinational enterprises suggests that their future competitive advantage may not reside in their strategy or structure, nor in their technologies or products, but in their organizational capabilities to cope with the multidimensional and complex demands of global business.
PAUL A. L. EVANS AND YVES DOZ[1]

The following questions represent substantive concerns of many managers who are involved with global cross-cultural business:

"We are redesigning our training programs for overseas assignees. Former assignees commented that they had difficulties in managing local employees and they hadn't prepared themselves. What kind of skills should we learn? Is it possible to learn a so-called global business sense?" (a human resources manager for a leading Japanese manufacturer)

"I'm in charge of a business unit of three hundred people and our company recently launched a worldwide operation. How should we proceed in order to make our business a success?" (a general manager of a fast-growing U.S. high-tech company)

"Last year we had a global retreat of key managers from all over the world. We tried to have lots of fun, but it didn't work. The Japanese participants in particular were extremely quiet.

What's wrong?" (a training director of a U.S. pharmaceutical company)

"Since we started the alliance with this Japanese company six months ago, I can't help thinking that we're wasting our time. So many meetings and videoconferences, but no progress. What should we do?" (an engineer with a U.S. telecommunications company)

Despite their efforts toward globalization, many managers today may feel uneasiness or frustration: they realize that they should do something but they are unsure why they cannot produce the results they wish to achieve. The common thread among them is a lack of awareness and understanding of the required competencies that result in globalization. As we have seen, more than ever before, strategic cultural intervention is a necessity for global corporations. In response to the question "What should we do?" this chapter outlines the heart of transcultural management: the five core competencies. They are:

1. The geocentric mindset
2. Strategic focus: the six Cs model
3. Cross-cultural communication skills
4. Culturally sensitive management processes
5. Synergy learning systems

Implementing the five competencies will provide an effective way to transform cultural clashes into cultural synergy and thus help organizations to become truly global companies. Each competency is indispensable, but it does not work alone because all five are interrelated (see Figure 5.1). This fact is critical, given that many managers are caught by the illusion that there is one, single right answer. Organizations have to realize the need for all of the competencies and actively embrace and promote them. Each competency is explained below.

The Geocentric Mindset

Although the geocentric mindset may also be termed a global mindset, in fact, it has broader meanings. Before sharing the differences as well as the commonalities, I will first define the global mindset.

Figure 5.1. The Five Core Transcultural Competencies.

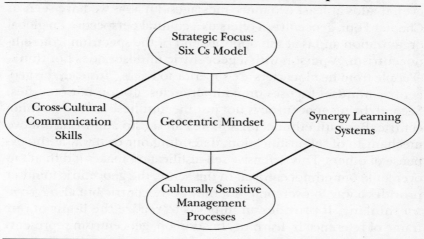

As Glenn Fisher wrote in his book, *Mindsets: The Role of Culture and Perception in International Relations,* mindsets are the mental attitudes formed by experience, education, prejudice, and other factors that predispose us to perceive and respond to situations in particular ways.[2] Thus, a mindset is a key element that affects the significance of psychological and cultural factors in international business situations. In a global mindset, as Stephen Rhinesmith explains, "we scan the world from a broad perspective, always looking for unexpected trends and opportunities that may constitute a threat or an opportunity to achieve our personal, professional, or organizational objectives."[3] As Percy Barnevik, the CEO of Asea Brown Boveri and a role model for the global mindset, clearly articulates:[4]

> Global managers have exceptionally open minds. They respect how different countries do things, and they have the imagination to appreciate why they do them that way. But they are also incisive, they push the limits of the culture. Global managers don't passively accept it when someone says, "You can't do that in Italy or Spain because of the unions" or "You can't do that in Japan because of the Ministry of Finance." They sort through the debris of cultural excuses and find opportunities to innovate. Global managers are also generous and patient. They can handle the frustrations of language barriers.

The geocentric mindset also shares these global features. However, it adds at least two more messages. First, as we have seen in Chapter Four, geocentrism offers us a cultural perspective on global organization and is at the opposite end of the spectrum from ethnocentrism. A person with a geocentric mindset does not think, "People from headquarters are superior to locals." Instead, the geocentric mindset focuses on competencies, not on nationalities. Second, being geocentric is not just the antithesis of being ethnocentric. Beneath ethnocentrism, we can see an almost instinctive mechanism of self-justification, defending our own way at the expense of others. This defensive self-justification makes it difficult to overcome our ethnocentrism. In this sense, the geocentric mindset provides a way to overcome not only ethnocentric but also *egocentric* thinking. It provides an impetus to realize the limits of our frame of reference by learning. In addition, geocentrism represents the other side of a continuum called "corporate-centrism."[5]

Hiroshi Okumura, a professor at Ryukoku University in Kyoto, defined corporate-centrism as the thought that corporations are more important than anything else, including individuals, stakeholders such as customers and shareholders, and society. It has been the major paradigm for most Japanese since World War II. The lifetime employment system, age-based promotion, and corporate cross-shareholding—in which major corporations hold stock of other major corporations in order to stabilize share price and enhance their relationships—have fostered the corporate-centric mindset. However, Japanese companies have recently begun to rethink the lifetime employment system and have broken the belief system that supported corporate-centrism. At the same time, we have seen the downside of corporate-centrism, such as the notorious *karoshi* syndrome (death caused by excess work), corporate crimes and scandals, and a lack of community and family responsibility. Corporate-centrism also has created global environmental problems. The Japanese are beginning to look for a postcorporate-centrism model. The answer lies in fostering a geocentric mindset through which we can become truly global citizens and in which the *geo* (the earth) comes before companies and nationalities.

The geocentric mindset is an attitude. We usually learn and unlearn attitudes subconsciously, and many of us have learned an ethnocentric or egocentric mindset without realizing it. In order to change our mindset, we have to reach the geocentric mindset by conscious learning through the other four competencies. Let us move on to the second competency.

Strategic Focus: The Six Cs Model

In conventional management theory, business strategy must take three main areas into account: the corporation, the customer, and the competitor, known as the "three Cs." After the Tokyo Stock Market meltdown in 1990, which caused the Japanese "bubble economy" to burst, Shintaro Hori, director and vice president of Bain & Co. in Japan, declared an end to a business environment where the three Cs model could adequately cover the key aspects of strategy.[6] According to Hori, the model needed a fourth C—*community*—because of the need for corporations to be socially responsible toward both domestic and international communities. Hori also mentioned the increasing contacts with host countries (for Japanese companies, host countries include the United States and Southeast Asian nations), a more diversified workforce, and an emerging concern for environmental issues.[7]

But even with community as a part of the strategic focus, we may remain unaware of what connects the other three parts of the strategic focus. The new strategic focus for transcultural management adds *communication,* which connects the other elements, and *culture,* which provides its context (see Figure 5.2). This expanded six Cs model more fully describes all aspects of national and organizational culture, the dynamics of multicultural organizations, international client relationships, and multinational public relations.

The need for the six Cs model of business strategy and the relationships between its parts are clear, except for one issue that may raise a question: Why does an organization need to communicate with its competitors? The answer is fairly straightforward. Communication with competitors ensures an accurate analysis of their strengths and weaknesses, especially across cultures. It also readies organizations for the possibility that, in today's complex and interconnected business environment, competitors quite often become strategic partners.

Companies that focus on customers, corporation, community, and competitors and ignore communication and culture as part of

Figure 5.2. The Six Cs Model.

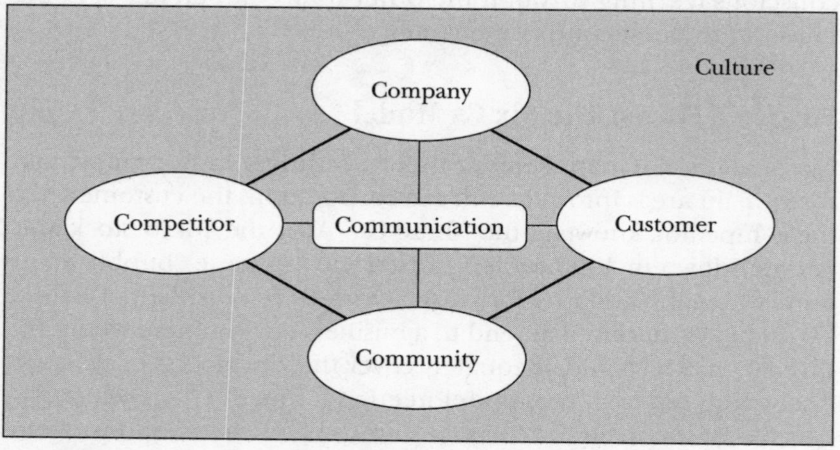

their strategic focus may find that they struggle in the multicultural environment and have difficulty in becoming global organizations. As we saw in Chapters One and Two, communication and culture may also act as blind spots despite their critical role. For instance, as an expert in multinational acquisition strategies reported, "Many companies today do a good job at due diligence, but they drop the ball after that. . . . They don't give much thought to an integration plan."[8] Integration requires mutual learning through communications among all managers and workers from different corporate and national cultures. It is not a easy job. The reality is that at least *half* of all cross-border acquisitions by multinational companies fail. Thus, cross-cultural communications, which is a skill that uses two components (culture and communication), is becoming even more important in the global workplace, and it is the third competency.

Cross-Cultural Communication Skills

Glenn Fukushima, who worked as a negotiator for five years in the difficult trade talks between U.S. Trade Representatives and the Japanese government in the late 1980s, said that poor communi-

cation was a major cause of the economic and political troubles between the two countries.[9] Since he was one of the few totally bilingual and bicultural officers involved in the U.S.–Japan trade talks,
he was able to see the critical role that cross-cultural communication played.

Similarly, the value of and need for cross-cultural communication skills cannot be overemphasized in organizational management. It is what enables any mission statement, vision, or strategy
to become a reality. Communications occur between individuals as
well as between organizations. An individual can communicate
with an organization and a social community through the media.
We also communicate through verbal vehicles (words) and various
nonverbal methods (gestures, facial expressions, or silence).
Whether we are conducting meetings or exchanging information,
we cannot do business without communication. But if communication is challenging in any business setting, it requires even more
attention to be efficient in situations where people from more than
one culture are attempting to work together.

In a lecture, Robert Moran, professor of international studies
and director of the Program in Cross-Cultural Communication at
the American Graduate School of International Management
(Thunderbird), quoted a phrase from Pascal's *Pensées:* "There are
truths on this side of the Pyrenees which are falsehoods on the
other." He also shared the following story:[10]

> About four years ago, I was giving a speech to a group of 50 or so
> Japanese bankers, many of whom were visiting the United States for
> the first time. Towards the end of my talk I illustrated a manage-
> ment concept from an example from our youngest child—then two
> years old. At the conclusion of my talk one person raised his hand
> and asked the following question: "Where does your child sleep?"
>
> I told him that our youngest child sleeps in a room called the
> nursery. "I think we Japanese love our children more than you
> Americans love your children," he responded. "I have two children,
> ages three and six. My three-year-old sleeps in the same room with
> me and my wife on the *tatami* mat floor. Whenever she wakes up at
> night, my wife gets up right away and attends to her needs. Perhaps
> that is why old people are in old-age homes in the United States—
> because you separate them as children."[11]

After telling this story, Moran drew two triangles and then split each triangle in half. He said, "In the first Pyrenees, this side is 'Sleep together with the baby' and another side is 'Sleep separately' [the factual description of this cultural practice]. In the second Pyrenees, this side is 'Love kids more' and the other side is 'Love kids less' [the conclusion the Japanese manager had drawn about the practice]. We cannot combine these two by using an equation" (see Figure 5.3).

This was a true *satori* (enlightened understanding) for me. Combining two "Pyrenees," one a factual statement and the other a subjective conclusion, as we often do, results in a judgment that in most cases is negative. In a cross-cultural work situation, we easily make these kinds of mistakes based on cultural preferences. For instance, a Japanese manager who gave a presentation to his American counterparts in the United States returned to Japan and told his colleagues that the Americans were rude and offensive. During his presentation, he received lots of questions from the Americans. Sometimes they interrupted him when asking questions. The Japanese manager, not used to this type of interaction, perceived the Americans as challenging him. He combined one "Pyrenees" (asking or not asking questions) with another (rude or not rude), thus drawing a false conclusion that when Americans ask questions they are being rude.

Figure 5.3. The Pyrenees of Cross-Cultural Communication.

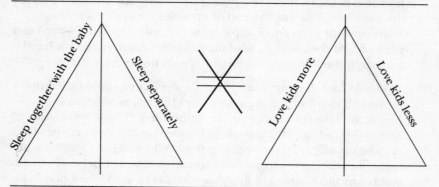

Source: Lecture by Robert Moran at the American Graduate School of International Management, February 1991. Used by permission of Robert Moran.

A fundamental skill for cross-cultural communicators is the ability to see behavior in its own right without making judgments or justifying their reactions. This is a key mental discipline for practicing the five core competencies of transcultural management.

Culturally Sensitive Management Processes

It is not difficult for businesspeople to list the pros and cons of multicultural organizations. As Robert Moran notes, the advantages usually include: a variety of different perspectives, which can foster creativity; diverse approaches to problem solving; a wider range of information; and an increase in knowledge and learning opportunities.[12] Disadvantages often include: communication difficulties, more time needed for meetings and tasks, linguistic difficulties, increased complexity, and negative stereotypes. Most people are able to discern both the advantages and the disadvantages. However, as Moran noted, when people were asked to list the disadvantages of working in a culturally diverse organization, they could do it in less than half the time it took them to list the advantages.[13] In other words, the disadvantages of cultural diversity are easy to recognize. Although people acknowledge the benefits of working in culturally diverse groups, they cannot easily access these benefits. The disadvantages are recognized and experienced more often, while the advantages are more conceptual and thus harder to experience.

How, then, can disadvantages be minimized and advantages be enhanced through management processes that retain cultural sensitivity? And how can these processes lead to greater workplace productivity? Nancy Adler describes group productivity as follows:[14]

Actual productivity = Potential productivity – Losses due to faulty process

Given this formula, we can see that if we can eliminate all the losses resulting from faulty process caused by cultural pitfalls, such as an inability to implement discussions, we can realize the full potential of multicultural work teams. Adler pointed out that multicultural groups have more potential for higher productivity than do homogeneous groups, but they also bear the risk of greater losses due to faulty process.[15]

To maximize productivity, we have to modify all the management processes according to the specific business and cultural environment and the skills, background, and experience of the group members (not only the résumés of the members but also their cross-cultural business expertise, relationships, and communication styles and the group culture). These management processes include planning, decision making, research, brainstorming, and meetings, as well as behaviors such as coaching, training, and interaction with customers. For example, Taylor Cox, Jr., associate professor of organizational behavior and human resources management at the University of Michigan, notes that U.S. brainstorming sessions are biased toward verbal fluency and monolingualism.[16] If the facilitator of a brainstorming session does not realize the institutionalized cross-cultural verbal impediments, then the session not only may be highly ineffective but also may create cultural clashes. In a country such as Japan where formality and hierarchy are important, *structured brainstorming* (where the facilitator acknowledges ideas in a structured way, for example, by seating participants in a certain way, taking comments according to the seating order, and not permitting interruptions) is more effective than the unstructured style common in the United States. Thus, along with the other four competencies of cross-cultural business management, knowing the specific cultural context enables management processes to be culturally sensitive and more effective.

Synergy Learning Systems

The notion of synergy is becoming another cliché in today's business environment. However, many people have a misconception about synergy—that it is something that occurs naturally. But this is not always the case. According to Robert Moran, "*Synergy in teams must be learned.* Furthermore, the issue is not just how the team can function more synergistically, but how it can integrate more effectively with the overall goals of the organization."[17] Otherwise, creating synergy is nothing but a slogan on the wall in the workplace.

As articulated by Robert Moran and Philip Harris, synergy is a dynamic process that involves two often-opposing views that must be brought together after both parties mutually conclude that they need to unite their efforts to achieve their goals and create an integrated solution.[18] Through combining action and working together, both parties bring or gain a true and complete understanding of both of their organizations and, especially, of each other's culture. The participants display empathy and sensitivity in interpreting each other's signals, with the result that the total effect is greater than the sum of their individual and independent actions. Synergy is sometimes illustrated by the analogy that 2 + 2 = 5 instead of 4, but given the various cross-cultural barriers, it may in fact look more like 2 + 2 = 3. In that case, the result is negative cultural synergy and no progress is made. Cultural synergy neither signifies compromise nor means that either party loses anything in the process. It exists only in relation to a practical set of circumstances and happens while people are doing something else that often has little to do with culture.

In reality, we often see negative cultural synergy. There is a sort of vicious circle where cultural issues act as blind spots for strategic planning and management decisions. Structures and systems become hindrances in cross-cultural organizations. For instance, both Japanese companies in the United States and American companies in Japan have difficulty coordinating the needs of each local business unit within subsidiaries in addition to their communications with the home office. As a result, interfunctional conflicts in headquarters (such as those between the research and development and marketing functions) are often boosted in local branches. In most cases, these organizations, which are suffering from negative cultural synergy, do not realize the root causes. Instead, they see cultural differences as obstacles.

In order to avoid such traps and create cultural synergy, the organization and its members must practice the four competencies we have discussed: the geocentric mindset, a strategic focus that includes culture and communication, cross-cultural communication skills, and culturally sensitive management processes. The organization then has to develop synergy learning systems that support the other four competencies at an organizational level. Synergy learning systems are institutionalized opportunities that promote mutual cross-cultural learning and that provide a feedback function that reflects the learning process. But how do organizations begin these opportunities? With the core element of synergy: learning the perspective of others. According to Stephen R. Covey:[19]

Valuing differences is the essence of synergy—the mental, the emotional, the psychological differences between people. And key to valuing those differences is to realize that all people see the world, not as it is, but as they are.

Providing institutionalized opportunities for cross-cultural learning to create synergy learning systems does not always mean providing "cultural training programs." They are necessary, but not sufficient. Once they return to work, participants in such cultural awareness and cultural sensitivity programs tend to forget all the learning because the programs rarely address issues that are directly related to their daily business. It is more important to *transform each cross-cultural work situation into a real-life cross-cultural action learning opportunity*. In each cross-cultural interaction, organizations must provide situations in which people can feel comfortable asking questions, receive feedback about their own interactions, and improve management operations through continuous cross-cultural learning.

For example, a successful U.S.–Japan joint venture company has been seriously learning cultural synergy. Both the Japanese and American managers are brushing up on their cross-cultural communication skills and are developing an understanding of their partner's technology, business philosophy, and management styles by taking a series of cross-cultural training programs that are mandatory for all "bridge" persons (those who bridge two cultures, such as expatriates, inpatriates, and frequent travelers). They regularly conduct cultural synergy meetings where they discuss a wide range of issues from a cross-cultural perspective: everything from strategy to meeting management. In some of the sessions, they compared their decision-making systems with each other and identified critical differences. For instance, the Japanese decision-making systems required more people and time than those of the Americans. After setting a common understanding, they tried to seek new rules. One outcome of the session was new rules for using E-mail: the Japanese were to clarify their logic and conclusions while the Americans were to demonstrate guidelines for communicating in international English. These rules defined a way to prioritize actions in response to requests. An organization that develops such synergy learning systems believes that cultural diversity is a strategic competency. It knows that it can foster creativity and improve productivity.

As we can see, the five core competencies are interrelated. Synergy learning systems can activate the other four competencies, but it is impossible for an organization to instill these systems without practicing the other four competencies. In short, it is critical to develop all five. Individuals and organizations can learn effectively, once they realize that the five core competencies make globalization possible. But it is also important not to rush toward instant perfection. How can we make globalization happen? Let us move into the actions to take in order to make the five core competencies a reality.

The Five Core Competencies in Action

A joint venture between an American high-tech company and a Japanese steel company was falling apart. Engineers from both companies had never gotten along. The American engineers, who were trained to be direct and confrontational, became frustrated with the Japanese engineers. According to an American manager, the Japanese group was reluctant to share information and was constantly indecisive: "They say, 'Yes, we can,' and come back after three weeks with 'No, we can't.'" On the other hand, the Japanese team thought that the American engineers did not have a good sense of teamwork. The senior Japanese engineer said, "We are not sure what they want to do as a team. In the meeting, they are always arguing among themselves." The two groups didn't exchange feedback on how they observed each other or try to find an alternative interpretation of their counterparts' behavior.

A joint venture between a fast-growing American company and a traditional Japanese company was beginning to work. Before they had signed their contract, the two parties had prepared themselves well. The American company, in particular, had anticipated some clashes with its Japanese partner because of their different styles and cultures. Compared to the Japanese partners, the Americans were more aware of the distinct characteristics of their corporate culture, such as an acceptance of risk taking and quick decision making. The joint steering committee of the two companies, which was charged with planning the initial work of the joint venture, listed potential downside areas and developed counterplans. One outcome was that a liaison team was set up to mediate conflicts between the two parties. For the first year, the liaison team analyzed all the complaints and categorized them into four major areas: interpersonal communications, meeting management, team management, and leadership. They invited key managers to off-site meetings and discussed the four areas in order to clarify cultural expectations and develop a mutual understanding. One American manager said, "I think we might reconsider our customary ready-fire-aim approach." A Japanese senior manager said, "We should change our traditional tapping-on-the-stone-bridge product development policy in order to keep up with today's competition."

It goes without saying that the first organization did not invest in the five core competencies, thinking it could not afford to care about cultural issues. It failed to engage in basic strategies such as exchanging feedback on how the two parties observed each other and seeking alternative interpretations of the other party's behaviors. The second organization did invest in the competencies and anticipated misunderstandings and potential conflict. Below are some strategies for putting the five core competencies into action.

Link the Five Competencies with Performance Appraisal

One effective way to promote the five core competencies is to link them with performance appraisal. For instance, General Electric Company's leadership values, which are the criteria for appraising managers, include a global mindset and diversity, vision, commitment, and integrity. By linking its performance appraisal systems with such values, GE is showing its employees that it is taking cultural issues seriously.

Fine-Tune All Communication

Given the preeminence of communication in transcultural management, it is crucial to pay acute attention to communication styles and fine-tune them according to each situation, whether it is a business-planning meeting, a videoconference, or an E-mail correspondence. Apply cross-cultural communication skills and cross-cultural meeting management techniques (see below). Become familiar with cultural context (covered in Chapter Seven) and nonverbal expressions. Practice international English as stated in Chapter Three. Be patient, refrain from quick judgments, and observe carefully.

Institute Cross-Cultural Meeting Management

Meeting management is crucial in cross-cultural situations and is a must-do action for creating cultural synergy. The following are essential techniques for managing cross-cultural meetings, which usually take twice as long as monolingual meetings. (These techniques also apply to video- and teleconferencing.)

Planning the Meeting

Planning a cross-cultural meeting requires more work and detailed attention than planning a monocultural meeting. The following issues need consideration:

1. *Note the title and function of participants.* Provide a list of meeting participants' names, titles, and functions. American groups often omit titles when providing a participant list to Japanese groups. Names and titles are important to the Japanese and they select their participants so that their titles and positions match those of the other (American) group.
2. *Anticipate the degree of linguistic proficiency.* It is crucial to provide information on participants' language ability. Do some homework; ask those who know members of the other group about their proficiency in English. Participants will then be prepared to speak the appropriate level of international English (see Chapter Three).
3. *Consider seating arrangements.* There is no one single best seating arrangement. It depends on the objectives of the meeting, the participants' language ability, the degree of formality, and so on. Consider the pros and cons and choose the best arrangement. For instance, the arrangement shown in Figure 5.4 is commonly used for a business-planning meeting. It helps the facilitator to guide the meeting according to the participants' range of linguistic abilities and allows everyone to take turns. On the other hand, unless it is carefully facilitated, this

Figure 5.4. Cross-Cultural Meeting Seating Arrangement A.

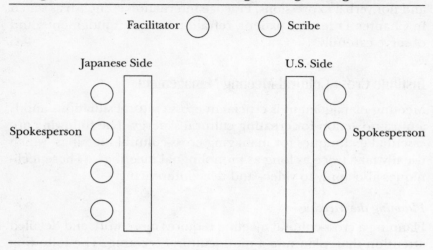

arrangement may promote an adversarial atmosphere. The arrangement in Figure 5.5 is used for a more informal meeting and is appropriate when fostering a buddy system. However, it requires some relationship building prior to the meeting. Otherwise the nonnative speakers (that is, the Japanese) are likely to stay quiet.

4. *Use free time strategically.* Socialization and break times can be used to maximize the effectiveness of the meeting. An appropriate break allows participants to discuss tough issues informally. For instance, for a one-day meeting, you may plan one break in the morning and two breaks in the afternoon. In general, determine breaks according to your group needs.

5. *Set the ground rules.* Send a description of the ground rules—guidelines on how the meeting will proceed—to all participants ahead of the meeting. Include an agenda, noting decisions to be made, and clarify the roles of all the participants.

Opening the Meeting

At the beginning of the meeting, the facilitator should state and clarify the following:

Figure 5.5. Cross-Cultural Meeting Seating Arrangement B.

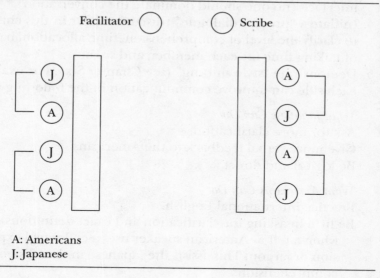

A: Americans
J: Japanese

1. Objectives
2. Procedures (agenda, scope of the issues, and so on)
3. Ground rules
4. The process for checking and summarizing (who will do this during the discussion, when, and how, in regard to the contents of the meeting)
5. The roles and functions of the meeting participants, for example, a scribe, an interpreter if necessary, a spokesperson for each party if necessary, and the participants themselves

During the Meeting

The facilitator or gatekeeper can help to keep everyone on track and focused in the following ways:

1. Make sure that people do not talk while other people are talking; it is especially important for participants to wait for the interpreter or scribe to finish interpreting or writing.
2. Control "side conversations." Designate a group for side conversations and announce when the side talks are over. Have the spokesperson summarize the contents of the side talks for the larger group.

3. Monitor the balance of time effectiveness and the quality of the interface (no one should dominate the conversation).
4. Initiate a "process dialogue" (discussed later in this chapter) to clarify the level of comprehension, time allocation, balance of talking time for each member, and so on.
5. Demonstrate "style shifting" (see Chapter Six). For example, each side can improve communication in the following ways:

What Japanese Can Do:
Ask for more clarification.
Give more verbal feedback to the Americans.
Be logical and direct.

What Americans Can Do:
Practice international English.
Be firm in asking for clarification and exact definitions when a fellow American speaker uses a colloquial expression or jargon. This assists the Japanese in their listening comprehension.
Be sensitive to the context, in addition to the content, of participants from high-context cultures (acknowledge nonverbal communication: not only what participants say but also how they say it).
Be patient.

After the Meeting

Sending out the minutes of the meeting, including action lists that indicate who is to do each task, and by what date, is basic. For cross-cultural meetings, this is an absolute must and cannot be skipped. In addition, it is important to keep communications open in case there are any follow-up comments or feedback from participants.

Use Cross-Cultural Task Forces

Many companies striving to be global organizations have established worldwide project teams in areas such as quality assessment, new-product development, and human resources development in order to share local knowledge and enhance global integration. But, in many cases, only headquarters staff members are active in these teams, while other national members passively receive directions from them. In order to avoid this passive situation, formulate a cross-national task force, starting in the planning stage by including key managers from overseas branches as active participants. Discuss with other national members their method of managing a task force, their expectations, and how long they may need in order to complete the task. Current communications tools such as E-mail and videoconferencing are helpful, but remember to apply international English to ensure the quality of communications.

Conduct Global Learning Opportunities

Some companies conduct global workshops; others conduct global business forums. What is common is that managers are invited from all overseas branches to knowledge-sharing and learning sessions. These are not just conventional training sessions that teach skills, but more participative sessions that promote interactions among all managers. Some companies use these sessions to discuss corporate vision. Others may conduct leadership development sessions. It is best to hold these sessions out of the home country in order to demonstrate global focus rather than having them be headquarters-driven events.

One of the most effective global learning exercises is *mindset mapping*. Mindset maps crystallize key value and belief systems by diagramming all aspects that influence the national mindset, including geographic, religious, and historical conditions as well as educational systems and the use of language. The mindset maps in Figures 5.6 and 5.7 were developed to describe Japan and the United States.

Once participants understand each national mindset, they can describe the global geocentric mindset by integrating the corporation's values, mission statements, and vision, thus enhancing global team building. Areas of discussion may include corporate history, work styles, norms, structures, systems, skills, and strategies that influence corporate culture. In this process, participants can determine whether their corporate values make sense in the global context. (See "Case 1: Global Workshop Conference" in the Appendix.)

Provide Built-In Cross-Cultural Team Development Opportunities

Team building for work units is an effective learning opportunity.[20] Team-building meetings usually cover such issues as team work styles, methods of handling conflict, team members' relationships, and team members' roles and functions. It is also possible to build team development sessions into regular business meetings, such as

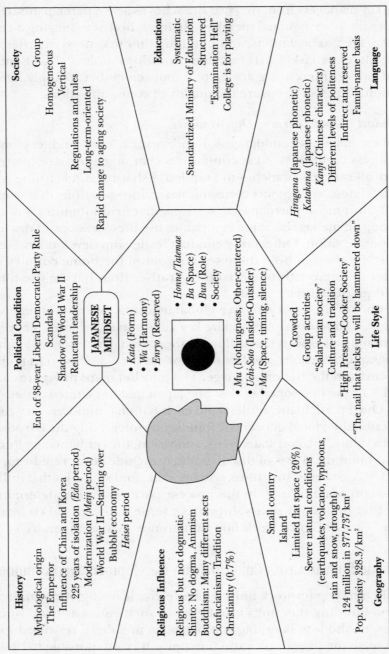

Figure 5.6. Japanese Mindset.

History

Mythological origin
The Emperor
Influence of China and Korea
225 years of isolation (*Edo* period)
Modernization (*Meiji* period)
World War II—Starting over
Bubble economy
Heisei period

Political Condition

End of 38-year Liberal Democratic Party Rule
Scandals
Shadow of World War II
Reluctant leadership

Society

Group
Homogeneous
Vertical
Regulations and rules
Long-term-oriented
Rapid change to aging society

Education

Systematic
Standardized Ministry of Education
Structured
"Examination Hell"
College is for playing

JAPANESE MINDSET

• *Kata* (Form)
• *Wa* (Harmony)
• *Enryo* (Reserved)

• *Homne/Tatemae*
• *Ba* (Space)
• *Bun* (Role)
• Society

• *Mu* (Nothingness, Other-centered)
• *Uchi-Soto* (Insider-Outsider)
• *Ma* (Space, timing, silence)

Religious Influence

Religious but not dogmatic
Shinto: No dogma, Animism
Buddhism: Many different sects
Confucianism: Tradition
Christianity (0.7%)

Geography

Small country
Island
Limited flat space (20%)
Severe natural conditions
(earthquakes, volcano, typhoons,
rain and snow, drought)
124 million in 377,737 km²
Pop. density 328.3/km²

Life Style

Crowded
Group activities
"Salary-man society"
Culture and tradition
"High Pressure-Cooker Society"
"The nail that sticks up will be hammered down"

Language

Hiragana (Japanese phonetic)
Katakana (Japanese phonetic)
Kanji (Chinese characters)
Different levels of politeness
Indirect and reserved
Family-name basis

Source: Geonexus Communications, Inc. Copyright © 1994 by Geonexus Communications, Inc. Reproduced by permission. Module developed with assistance from Matt Turowshi and Dr. Jean Wilcox.

Figure 5.7. U.S. Mindset.

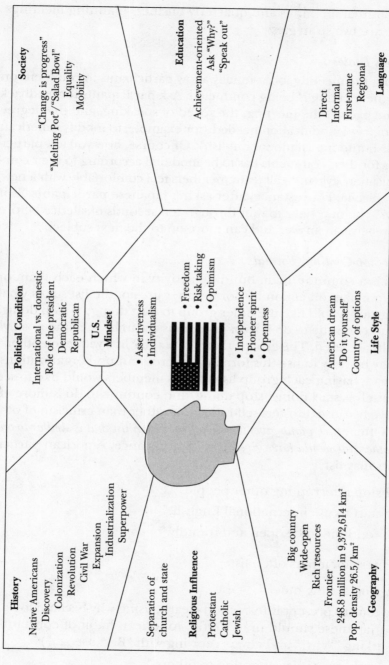

Political Condition
International vs. domestic
Role of the president
Democratic
Republican

Society
"Change is progress"
"Melting Pot"/"Salad Bowl"
Equality
Mobility

Education
Achievement-oriented
Ask "Why?"
"Speak out"

History
Native Americans
Discovery
Colonization
Revolution
Civil War
Expansion
Industrialization
Superpower

U.S. Mindset

- Assertiveness
- Individualism

- Freedom
- Risk taking
- Optimism

- Independence
- Pioneer spirit
- Openness

Language
Direct
Informal
First-name
Regional

Religious Influence
Separation of
church and state
Protestant
Catholic
Jewish

Geography
Big country
Wide-open
Rich resources
Frontier
248.8 million in 9,372,614 km²
Pop. density 26.5/km²

Life Style
American dream
"Do it yourself"
Country of options

Source: Geonexus Communications, Inc. Copyright © 1994 by Geonexus Communications, Inc. Reproduced by permission. Module developed with assistance from Matt Turowshi and Dr. Jean Wilcox.

semiannual meetings and quarterly business-planning meetings. Here are two strategies:

Process Dialogue

During the meeting, occasionally allow participants to comment on how the meeting is being conducted. Ask participants for feedback on the pace of the meeting, the speed of speaking, and the degree of language modification needed (for example, to modify American English into international English). Of course, how you ask participants for their comments has to be modified according to their communication style until all team members feel comfortable with a new, shared style. For instance, after asking Japanese participants "Is it okay?" you may have to wait through ten seconds of silence before you receive an answer and can move on to the next subject.

Start-Stop-Continue Format

This is a common team-building activity in which each team or group makes an action list for another group; the list states what the group would like the other group to start doing, to stop doing, and to continue to do if its expectations are to be met and positive results achieved. The groups then share their lists with each other.[21] It may be risky to use this format with cross-cultural organizations. Instead, having each group list what its members would like to see themselves start doing, stop doing, and continue to do is more effective because it fosters self-reflection rather than criticism of others. Often, *each group gives themselves an action list that is similar to one the other side would have given them.* For instance, American participants may list:

"We stop interrupting other people."

"We start to use international English."

"We continue to be open and friendly."

Japanese members often list:

"We stop staying quiet."

"We start to present information clearly, using why-because logic."
   (Japanese should practice the American habit of constantly asking "Why?" and always replying with "Because . . .")

"We continue to pay attention to others."

Develop Skilled Cross-Cultural Process Facilitators

A cross-cultural process facilitator is a staff member or consultant who can manage multicultural meetings and business processes in the most effective way. According to Mary O'Hara-Devereaux and Robert Johansen, he or she is "an active player in the same processes through which he or she is guiding a team—whether it be forging shared understandings in a multicultural context, mastering remote communications, devising systems of consensus decision making, or creating and maintaining a sense of team identity."[22] Cross-cultural process facilitators have the following specific skill set, in addition to the five core competencies:

1. *Helicopter thinking:* "Helicoptering" means zooming up and down so that you can see the whole picture as well as the details.[23] A cross-cultural facilitator has to see both the forest and the trees. To do so, the facilitator must know the direction and the scope of the discussion topic and constantly balance them with the content of the meeting.
2. *Submarine observation:* As we saw in Chapter Two, working across cultures requires seeing more than just the surface. "Submarine observation" is looking at the cultural traits at work below sea level (see Figure 2.2, the dual iceberg model). It is critical to be able to see the values and belief systems operating through various behaviors.
3. *Multilingual skills:* If the meeting is bicultural (for example, between the United States and Japan), ideally the facilitator should have bilingual facilitating competencies. If the group contains members from more than two national cultures, it helps to have a multilingual facilitator. When the facilitator speaks the participants' home language, receptivity for all is enhanced.

Develop and Embrace Bridge Persons

Bridge persons know more than one national culture, as either expatriates, inpatriates, or frequent travelers, and have cross-cultural business skills. They provide cross-cultural insight on specific business issues. If organizations acknowledge their value and embrace and use their skills, they can contribute immensely to a cross-cultural learning organization and act as catalysts in creating cultural synergy.

Some companies, such as Nestlé, have a position called "international personnel."[24] Those assigned to this position do not belong to a specific country or region. Instead, they spend half of their career outside the Swiss headquarters, developing and sharing their multicultural business expertise. (See Chapter Thirteen for an expanded discussion of bridge persons.)

Chapter Six

Achieving Competency
Seven Mental Disciplines

When you learn a discipline itself, you may find pain.
However, when you start learning something through the
discipline, you will find pleasure.
A MARTIAL ARTIST

Can we really attain a geocentric mindset? Can we communicate
across cultures effectively? Can we really create true cultural synergy? It is not an easy task to develop and implement the five core
competencies. There are many challenges. The first is to understand the two critical patterns of cross-cultural interaction, a vicious
circle of blame and a virtuous circle of learning, and to place ourselves within the virtuous circle. Also crucial to achieving transcultural competency are the seven mental disciplines. Where the five
core competencies are generally practiced on an institutional level,
the mental disciplines work on a more individual, internal level.

The Vicious and Virtuous Circles
of Cross-Cultural Interaction

By knowing how we start the trap of blaming others, we can avoid
it and shift to constructive interactions. When we look closely at individual behavior in a cross-cultural working environment, we tend
to find either a vicious circle or a virtuous circle. In both patterns,
intention, information, and interaction are vital elements.

Those caught in the vicious circle (Figure 6.1) are reluctant to work with people from different cultures and may be very distrustful. They tend to think, "Why do I have to work with those foreigners? I don't trust them." Their intentions are to avoid or minimize cross-cultural exposures. They may be influenced by limited, stereotyped, and biased information; as a result, they focus on the difficult aspects or problems in the interaction. They may reinforce their convictions and negative images with quick judgments, such as "As I expected, those foreigners are sly. That's why I can't trust them." Then they reconfirm their belief that they may be better off not dealing with foreigners. This kind of vicious circle, although it begins at an individual level, grows like a snowball and often causes an organizational avalanche of distrust and an ensuing crisis.

On the other hand, the intention of those in a virtuous circle (Figure 6.2) leans toward curiosity. They say, "I'm curious about how they do business." Curiosity leads to a desire to learn. Since these people want to learn about other cultures, they are interested in wide-open information, beyond negative stereotypes. As a result, they can use each interaction as a learning opportunity and get feedback from their experience that enriches both curiosity and knowledge. Observations are open-minded, such as "I thought they

Figure 6.1. A Vicious Circle of Cross-Cultural Interaction.

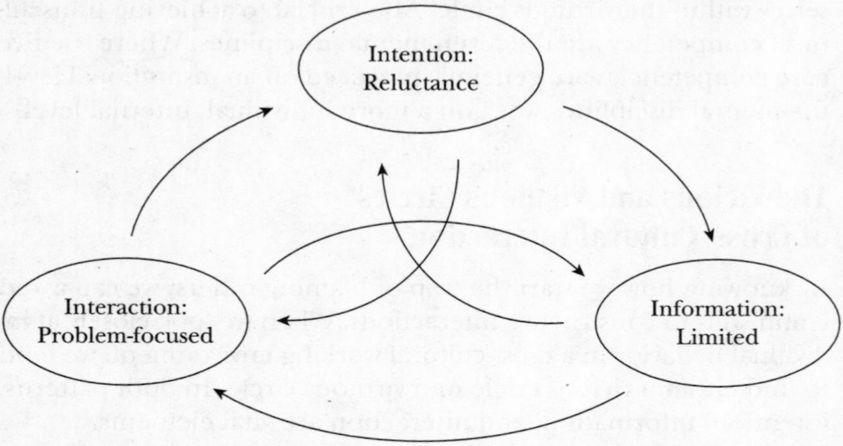

were rude, but I realized that it was only my different expectations." In this way, they develop a sense of trust.

No one wants to stay in a vicious circle. However, people may be unconsciously trapped by job pressures, frustration, and a hectic workload. Then the internal negative dialogue may begin. In order to prevent this trap, we first have to develop an awareness of our own patterns of vicious dialogue. If we pay attention to these vital elements of intention, information, and interaction, a shift from a vicious circle to a virtuous circle can happen. If not, the reverse shift can easily take place. Even someone who is open-minded may encounter an unpleasant experience and leap to a negative stereotype, thus triggering a vicious circle.

The Seven Mental Disciplines

There are many appropriate descriptions of the personal traits and skills needed to work effectively across cultures. I'd like to summarize seven mental disciplines that are necessary to do this. Although the five core competencies are designed for organizations and individuals, the seven mental disciplines focus on individuals, especially on our intrapersonal dialogues and reactions.

Figure 6.2. A Virtuous Circle of Cross-Cultural Interaction.

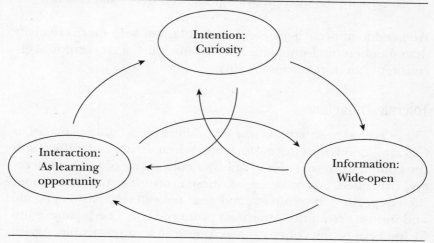

Observe the Situation Without Judgments

Observation without judgment is one of the most difficult disciplines. Since we are raised and trained to make judgments, we constantly make evaluations. Although we may withhold a judgment for a moment, we eventually have to make an evaluation. For instance, the Japanese "dead-fish" handshake is often uncomfortable to other international businesspeople and may give a weak or distrustful impression. However, as you observe carefully, leaving behind initial judgments, you may understand that the Japanese are simply trying to be polite, gentle, and respectful.

In learning this discipline, it is important to approach each situation with a nonjudgmental observation in order to maximize input, learn about others, and minimize biases and preconceptions. Try to notice your own use of adjectives, such as *good, bad, right,* and *wrong.* Then withhold that judgment and observe carefully. Observation without judgment is not only important in cross-cultural interactions; it also enhances our creativity. According to Michael Ray and Rochelle Myers in their book, *Creativity in Business:*[1]

> Even a slight decrease in judgment increases your ability to respond creatively to situations. It has been estimated that a normal individual uses only five percent of his total capability. We blame that on the VOJ (Voice of Judgment). If, by silencing the VOJ even a bit, you reclaim only an additional five percent of your total mental capacity, you will *double* your present efficiency and creativity.

We need to approach cross-cultural situations with more creativity than monocultural situations. At the same time, a cross-cultural encounter is an impetus for creativity.

Tolerate Ambiguity

There are many situations when working across cultures makes us feel ambiguous and uncomfortable. When we are unfamiliar with the communication styles of another culture, we often feel uneasy and frustrated. For instance, Japanese nonverbal communication, such as posture, eye contact, and gestures, often seems very subtle and indirect from the American point of view. The Japanese unfocused eye contact often annoys American businesspeople. Again, as with handshaking, the Japanese are trying to be polite and respectful. In many Asian and Middle Eastern countries, direct eye contact is perceived as offensive, rude, or a direct challenge. In order to tolerate ambiguity and learn what is beneath the surface, we have to practice *patience*. Patience builds trust. According to a former expatriate who lived in Japan for five years and achieved remarkable success in his Japanese operation, "There are three keys to doing business in Japan: First, patience. Second, absolute patience. Third, committed patience." Patience and perseverance always count. As Stephen Covey writes, "Negative synergy is an enormous waste of human talent. The formula for positive synergy is involvement + patience = commitment."[2] Working across cultures always requires a stronger commitment as well as patience.

Practice Style Shifting

Style shifting is the ability to expand our own views, styles, and thought patterns and choose the appropriate style according to the situation. It is a significant skill to be able to adjust your style—whether in communication, leadership, or negotiation—in situations where you are interacting with people from different cultures. The key is to learn the other people's cultural values and communication styles. Japanese communication styles tend to be more indirect and formal than American styles. One American expatriate manager performs style shifting well. Although she is a high-powered, fast speaker, she softens her voice with Japanese clients and becomes patiently silent.

A key challenge in style shifting is finding an appropriate degree of behavior. For example, some Japanese who speak English quite well and who wish to adopt a more casual American style may tend toward the opposite extreme and become too direct in their communications, even by American standards. They are unable to sense the appropriate level of directness and informality. Many American expatriates and visitors are surprised by the resulting questions from their Japanese colleagues, such as "How much salary do you receive?" Likewise, some American visitors to Japan make their counterparts uncomfortable by demonstrating excessive formality in their bowing and exchange of business cards. Needless to say, it is important to gauge the degree of style shifting that is appropriate.

Flip Your Perception

Perception flipping takes place when you assume the other person's perception of events, situations, or people. Before criticizing someone's behavior, it helps to flip your perception and see her or his point of view. After doing this, people often acknowledge, "I never thought of that." For example, a Japanese manager transferred to a U.S. branch office kept his office door closed, whereas the former Japanese manager had practiced an open-door policy. Some American subordinates started feeling uncomfortable and wondered why he was so secretive. In fact, the new Japanese manager had last worked in Germany, where it was considered sloppy to keep your door open. He was simply continuing this habit.

Reprogram Your Questions

If we ask ourselves, "How can they be so rude?" or "Why is he insensitive?" we have made a negative presupposition. If we instead ask, "What is the reason behind his behavior?" we avoid being trapped in our own assumptions, thereby allowing us to explore the other person's frame of reference without bias. Many people know that asking questions opens us to problem solving and creativity, but *questioning our own questions is even more vital.* It is a discipline that complements those of avoiding value judgments and tolerating ambiguity.

Reprogramming questions is a continual discipline. For example, a Japanese engineer visiting his joint venture partner in Silicon Valley initially complained, "Why are American workers so irresponsible? They are not working after 5:00 P.M. I don't see anyone." He didn't ask himself, "Why don't I see my American colleagues after 5:00?" or "Is there a reason?" But after two weeks, he found out that the Americans started working at 7:00 or 7:30 A.M., which explained why they "left early" according to his preconceived notion. An American controller assigned to a Japanese subsidiary shared his experience. His company was selling computers in the Japanese market, and he observed Japanese employees repackaging computers into new cardboard boxes. He thought it was a waste of time and materials. Immediately he reprogrammed his question from "Why are they doing so much extra work?" to

"What's the reason behind the work?" Shortly after, he noticed that all the original boxes had some dents or dirt. He remembered that Japanese consumers care not only about the contents (the computer) but also about the context (the packaging).

Work Interdependently

We all know the importance of interdependency and interconnectedness with other countries, organizations, and people. We know about the illusion of being independent as well as the drawbacks of codependency. Cultural synergy never happens when one culture dominates others. For the concept of interdependency, however, it is difficult to share the same meanings and nuances across cultures. In particular, the Japanese people, whose cultural traits are group-oriented and relationship-based, may have a different definition of interdependency. For instance, many American business travelers to Japan tend to be overwhelmed by Japanese hospitality. They may be frustrated or somewhat smothered by all the attention. They may need a break and prefer to return to their hotel rooms rather than be "taken care of" by their Japanese host. On the other hand, Japanese visitors to the United States often feel that they are not treated as they would expect to be in Japan, making them feel taken for granted rather than like a special guest.

In order to work interdependently as a team, it is critical to observe the relationship with your partner and clarify each expectation. One cross-cultural task force of a research and development division at a Japan branch office of an American company identified specific team-guiding principles to ensure their daily team behaviors:

- *Team objectives:* Our team objective is to provide the most innovative product concept by synergizing our diverse expertise.
- *Team value:* Our team values each professional individual. Thus, we constantly develop ourselves and respect others' expertise.
- *Team participation:* Our team expects each individual to participate equally in discussions, decisions, and our team commitment to the project.

- *Team communication:* Our team believes that high-quality communication creates high-quality outcome. Thus, we practice clear, direct, but heartfelt communication.

Keep Mental Stability and Growth

Working across cultures produces stress, both physical and mental. Speaking different languages, traveling, and adjusting communication modes are not easy jobs. We have to develop a mental toughness and take each situation as an opportunity for our own personal growth. Some people practice stress management and relaxation. Others look for philosophical or spiritual foundations. It is important to find our own ways to keep ourselves stable and to grow. One way to practice this discipline is to have a belief that we can always learn and enjoy our journey—a journey of crossing the divide.

Crossing the Divide: A Joy of the Journey

It is easy to say, "Be nonjudgmental and tolerant of ambiguity." However, our challenge is to control the automatic, instinctive, and relentlessly defensive mechanism called self-justification. That is why the above guidelines are called mental *disciplines*, rather than skills. As Peter Senge wrote about discipline:[3]

> By "discipline," I do not mean an "enforced order" or "means of punishment," but a body of theory and technique that must be studied and mastered to be put into practice. A discipline is a developmental path for acquiring certain skills or competencies. As with any discipline, from playing the piano to electrical engineering, some people have an innate "gift," but anyone can develop proficiency through practice. To practice a discipline is to be a lifelong learner. You "never arrive"; you spend your life mastering disciplines.

We can start practicing these disciplines in many of our daily activities. For example, I was forced to practice several of the mental disciplines in the following nonbusiness situation that involved eating grapes. Americans and Europeans usually eat a grape by putting it into their mouth, skin and all. The Japanese, however, eat grapes by separating the grape skin from the grape, either by peeling it off with their fingers or by putting it into their mouth, popping out the flesh, and then removing the skin.

I realized this difference while I was traveling in France. I was staying at the home of friends, a French couple and their ten-year-old daughter. One day they served grapes, and I started eating them the Japanese way. The girl pointed at me, started laughing, and said something to her parents. Although I do not speak French, I could tell that she was saying something like "Look how strange he is, taking the skin out of his mouth like that!" From my side, their popping the grapes into their mouths and eating them whole seemed unsanitary because the skins might be covered with pesticides. But then I was able to see myself through their eyes and understand how awful my manners must have looked. I started eating as they did. Then I realized that the skin of their French grapes was thinner than the skin of Japanese grapes, and so I could start to enjoy their way of eating.

The process I went through is described by Milton Bennett as the "six stages of intercultural sensitivity." According to his theory, I went through the first stages of denial, defense, and minimization of difference.[4] But then the situation shifted dramatically as I went through the last three stages: acceptance, adaptation, and integration. Bennett points out the paradigmatic divide that separates the first three ethnocentric stages from the latter three stages. When we cross the divide, we change our perception completely. In my case, the honest feedback from the ten-year-old girl made me cross the divide.

In the multicultural global work environment, we may have to cross many divides. Some of them are easy to cross and others are not. The five competencies and the seven mental disciplines help us to challenge those divides. Sometimes, we are required to travel extra miles. However, the journey is worthwhile for those who can enjoy new discoveries.

Chapter Seven

Managing the Cultural Context

The way we perceive is much more locked on than we realize.
GLEN FISHER[1]

The five core competencies and the seven mental disciplines provide guidelines that make it possible to achieve transcultural management, in which appropriate and effective management behaviors and styles are applied across cultures. Successful global managers also need to be able to understand a new or different cultural context and to respond to it effectively. In some situations, there may be time to study and plan for a given cultural context, but on other occasions, we may find ourselves having to respond immediately and with little preparation. By understanding several key cultural styles such as *tatemae* (facade), *honne* (reality), and the high-context model, managers and employees can communicate and work more smoothly with others in the global workplace. This chapter examines useful theories and research on cultural context and then shows how to apply the resulting insights to particular business situations.

Cross-Cultural Communication: Dealing with *Tatemae* and *Honne*

In his article, "What's So New About the New Economy?"[2] Alan Webber, the former editorial director of the *Harvard Business Review,* best described the role of communication in the emerging knowledge-based business society:

In the new economy, conversations are the most important form of work. Conversations are the way knowledge workers discover what they know, share it with their colleagues, and in the process create new knowledge for the organization. The panoply of modern information and communications technologies—for example, computers, faxes, e-mail—can help knowledge workers in this process. But it all depends on the quality of the conversations that such technologies support.

Webber and others send an important message: "In the end, conversation comes down to trust."[3] The trust-building process depends on the quality of the conversation, which is equal to the quality of the communication. This point is crucial—especially in regard to the quality of cross-cultural conversation—but it is one that we often forget. If we did remember it, we would not have to hear the following classic story over and over again.

A U.S. manager, visiting Japan to promote a product, told his Japanese colleague, a marketing manager, to arrange a visit to a customer. The Japanese manager, knowing that the style of the U.S. manager was too aggressive for the Japanese, was unwilling to arrange the visit to the client. However, he felt that he had to arrange the meeting and they visited the client together. The Japanese client was courteous to the American visitor and responded to his requests in a diplomatic way (saying, "Yes, yes," and nodding). In other words, the answer this client gave the U.S. manager was no more than a *tatemae* (a facade, what is supposed to be said). But the U.S. manager took this *tatemae* literally and returned to U.S. headquarters with a positive sense of achievement. Meanwhile, his Japanese colleague received a phone call from the client, who said, "Never bring that kind of guy to see me again!" This message never reached the U.S. manager, because his Japanese colleague didn't want to offend him.

This pattern can also often be seen when an American representative visits the Ministry of Finance (MOF) or the Ministry of Health and Welfare (MHW) to get approval for a new product. Even though the MOF and MHW officers are in the top echelons of the Japanese business hierarchy and have a lot of experience dealing with foreign representatives, they still sometimes only show their *tatemae* to the American executives. As a result, their comments can easily mislead the American visitors, who may have been waiting for new-product approval for as long as two years.

After these stories were relayed to a group of American managers, one of them commented, "We are not that simple. What you are saying makes us look like fools." Then another manager quickly said, "Yeah, but this is very typical. I know one guy who had exactly this experience." Many expatriates and visitors prepare themselves by studying the Japanese language and Japanese business practices. They may know what *tatemae* and *honne* are. However, it is often difficult to apply this cognitive knowledge in practice. In addition, *we often listen only to what we want to hear.* Those who are under pressure from headquarters tend to tune in to the positive news, whether it is *tatemae* or not.

These problems are caused not only by American visitors who do not know Japanese business practices and customs, but also by their Japanese colleagues who do not know how to give constructive and logical feedback or to strategize with Americans. Neither have learned how to handle cross-cultural conversations. How do you work with *tatemae* and *honne? Tatemae* is a reality and should not be denied, but you can work with it rather than against it. In order to avoid this type of communication problem, which prevents us from establishing the trust-based conversations that are so essential to the new economy, we have to develop our knowledge of the function of cultural contexts and learn how to apply cross-cultural communication skills.

Ascribed Context and Achieved Content

Edward T. Hall's high-context and low-context model helps to explain the source of miscommunication between U.S. headquarters and their Japanese subsidiaries.[4] A high-context communication or message is one in which most of the information is already encoded within the person, while very little is coded in the explicit, transmitted part of the message. For example, in the above instance of the American manager, the Japanese paid more attention to the situation, their relationship with the Japanese client, and *how* the Japanese client said "yes" rather than to the client's actual words. A low-context communication is just the opposite. The American manager took the Japanese client's "yes" literally, without regard for the context in which it was given.

The Japanese communication style is categorized as high-context and low-content, while the American communication style is low-context and high-content. When an American communicates with another American, they focus on the content (A-n in Figure 7.1[5]) rather than the context (A-x). American parents often tell their children, "Tell it like it is." When Japanese communicate, they focus on the context (J-x) rather than the content (J-n). When an American tries to communicate with a Japanese without changing communication styles, the amount of information the Japanese will receive based on the content (J-n) is much less than if he or she were an American using the American low-context communication style.

It is very difficult to read cultural context when communicating with people from different cultures. The classic example of cross-cultural miscommunication between the U.S. manager and his Japanese customer described above occurred because of this fact, and therefore the American experienced a wide communication gap (A-n minus J-n). If the American manager had realized the importance of context, he could have approached the Japanese client more appropriately. For instance, to show respect to the client, the American manager could have apologized for the sudden visit and could have shown appreciation for the client's past business to reinforce the relationship, because relationship is context.

Figure 7.1. Context and Content.

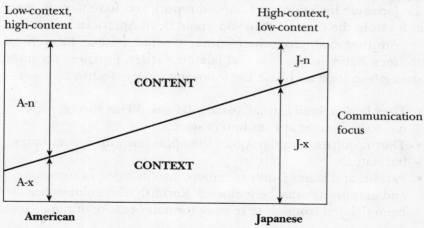

Low-context, high-content

High-context, low-context

CONTENT

CONTEXT

A-n

A-x

J-n

J-x

Communication focus

American   **Japanese**

The high-context communication style is deeply ingrained in the Japanese mindset. Some often-quoted proverbs that the Japanese value exemplify the high-context style of communication:

Silence is golden.

Still water runs deep.

A wise man hears one and understands ten.

A wise hawk hides his talons.

The high- and low-context model also explains some critical cross-cultural management issues beyond individual stylistic differences. Regarding differences in marketing research, Johny K. Johansson and Ikujiro Nonaka wrote:[6]

> Japanese companies want information that is context specific rather than context free—that is, data directly relevant to consumer attitude about the product, or to the way buyers have used or will use specific products, rather than research results that are too remote from actual consumer behavior to be useful.

In short, Japanese market researchers take context into account more than content, such as quantified market research data. In addition, non-Japanese may find financial annual reports difficult to read. Some say that understanding the gray areas of Japan's financial reporting can be more important than knowing the actual tax regulations.[7] In other words, because the content is so limited in the Japanese high-context financial report, you have to read even more from the content than you would in an American report.

Another example is the résumé, in which critical differences are seen between the U.S. and Japanese styles. Japanese résumés are high-context and have the following unique features:

- They have a fixed format, usually B4 size. (This special paper has to be bought at a stationery store.)
- They require a photograph of the applicant with age and marital status.
- Parents and other family members' names, ages, occupations, and employers must be included. Recently, this column has been deleted from some résumé formats because of the

emerging awareness of discrimination. However, the majority still use the conventional format.

- There is no room to write about specific achievements, only the names of the organizations to which the applicant has belonged.
- Expressions such as "I was responsible for," "I achieved," and "I handled," typical in U.S. résumés, are not considered appropriate.

A study by Fons Trompenaars explains the contrast in style between U.S. and Japanese résumés. One of the key dimensions of cultural difference he found is the difference between *achieved* status and *ascribed* status: "While some societies accord status to people on the basis of their achievements, others ascribe it to them by virtue of age, class, gender, education and so on."[8] His survey shows that the United States, Canada, and Norway are achievement-oriented cultures. At the other end of the spectrum are countries influenced by Catholicism, Buddhism, and Hinduism, including Italy, Mexico, France, China, Indonesia, and Japan.[9] Most of the ascribed countries are high-context cultures. (Figure 7.2. positions countries within the high- and low-context model.) Unless we know the social context of a résumé, we cannot understand much from its content.

The high- and low-context model clearly indicates the reasons for long-standing misunderstandings and communication difficulties. A cross-cultural perspective can shed light. Up to the 1980s, countries that held hegemonic power were all low-context countries, for example, Holland, the United Kingdom, and the United States. Japan is the first high-context country that has achieved economic success on a global scale. From the perspective of a low-context country, content, such as economic data and product information, is most visible and therefore available for consideration. Contextual issues are seldom understood or interpreted accurately, which is why many Western books and articles that try to explain the Japanese economic miracle tend to propagate an extreme image of the Japanese as aggressive, predatorial capitalists or as having a superproductive system. The elements regarded as the strengths that led to Japanese economic power, such as government intervention, a high educational infrastructure, and other

Figure 7.2. Position of Nationalities in the High- and Low-Context Model.

High Context

Japanese
Chinese
Arab
Greek
Mexican
Spanish
Italian
French
French Canadian
English
English Canadian
American
Scandinavian
German
Swiss-German

Low Context

Source: Adapted from Gary P. Ferraro, "Ibunka Management," in K. Enatsu and M. Ohta, eds., *The Cultural Dimension of International Business* (Tokyo: Dobunkan, 1992), pp. 102–103.

cultural aspects (for example, group efforts that easily create teamwork and a work ethic influenced by Confucianism), surely contributed to its success. However, one point that is often overlooked is that these elements all fit well in a certain stage of economic development: the era of standardized mass production. Now that Japan faces a new economic stage—one that is not based on mass production—Japanese companies are struggling (see Chapter Eleven).

Western experts on Japan have to recognize the cultural variables that influence their research and observations. At the same time, Japan has to be more explicit in describing the context in which information is presented in order to prevent misunderstanding and isolation from the rest of the world.

Cross-Cultural, Multidimensional Research

Most theories and models have their advantages and their disadvantages—so, too, does the high- and low-context model. One drawback is that it is based on a single dimension: differences in communication style. In addition, quantitative and multinational research data on the model are insufficient. Cultural research tends to become qualitative, but quantitative information is also critical for specific cultural interventions such as organization development or diagnosis of corporate culture. We need to know not only what is similar and what is different, but also just how different things are, based on statistical evidence. In addition, because of the expanding global business environment, we need multinational data.

One of the most reliable cross-cultural management studies was made by Geert Hofstede. It covers all of the above requirements. His research included 116,000 questionnaires from IBM group employees in fifty different countries and three regions.[10] While some may argue that the study only reflects the parameters of IBM corporate culture, Hofstede used matched samples (that is, the samples were similar in all respects—education, gender, age, and type of work organization—except nationality) and identified national cultural differences even among IBM people.[11]

Hofstede identified five dimensions where significantly different management styles and belief systems were observed. The first is labeled "individualism versus collectivism."[12] In a high-individualism society, the ties between individuals are very loose, whereas in a low-individualism society, the ties are strong. The second is "power distance,"[13] which indicates how a society deals with inequalities among people. A high-power-distance society tends to formulate hierarchical social structures, whereas a low-power-distance society encourages the idea that everyone has equal rights. The third is "uncertainty avoidance,"[14] defined as the extent to which the members of a culture feel threatened by uncertain or unknown situations. A high-uncertainty-avoidance society accepts familiar risks but fears ambiguous situations and unfamiliar risks, whereas a low-uncertainty-avoidance society is comfortable with unfamiliar risks.

The fourth dimension is "masculinity versus femininity,"[15] which indicates the division of roles between men and women in society. A high-masculinity society has clear distinctions in gender roles; that is, men are supposed to be assertive, tough, and focused on material success, whereas women are supposed to be more modest, tender, and concerned with the quality of life. A low-masculinity (or femininity) society has overlapping gender roles. The fifth dimension is "long-term orientation."[16] A high-long-term-orientation society accepts that it may take a long time to get results, whereas a low-long-term-orientation society expects quick results (see Figure 7.3).

Given these five dimensions, Japan belongs in the group of collective, high-power-distance, high-uncertainty-avoidance, masculine, and long-term-orientation societies; the United States belongs to the more individualistic, low-power-distance, low-uncertainty-avoidance, masculine, and short-term-orientation societies (see Table 7.1). Except for the masculinity-versus-femininity index, which shows that both the United States and Japan are strong achievement- and success-oriented cultures, the two countries are diametrically opposed. This study statistically validates much of the literature on the United States and Japan that tries to explain the cultural differences between the two countries. In addition to the context-content model, this research also demonstrates why it is difficult for the United States to get a correct picture of Japan.

Furthermore, using this cross-cultural, multidimensional research, we can see other crucial points that do not appear in single-dimensional models such as the high- and low-context model. First, the order of countries varies according to the dimension being analyzed. In other words, countries can be different in different ways, which is just common sense. However, many people fail to recognize this as common sense. As one Western author wrote, "Japanese are different from those elsewhere in the world, especially from Americans,"[17] and many Japanese also propagate the "we are unique" syndrome, saying "Japan is different from your country." Tsuneo Iida, professor of international Japanese cultural research, pointed out this Japanese "panda syndrome": "We have said too much that we are like the panda—we live in a different world and are unique creatures."[18] This self-regard perpetuates isolation and misunderstanding.

Second, multidimensional research indicates the *degree of differences and similarities*. Many scholars (especially the well-known Chie Nakane in her book, *Japanese Society*[19]) address the vertical structure of Japanese society and overemphasize the hierarchical nature of the culture, even though more than 80 percent of Japanese believe that they are middle class. In addition, in Japanese corporations, the horizontal network of connections known as *doki* (same year of entering a school or organization) plays a major role in the day-to-day functioning of businesses. On the power-distance index (PDI), Japan's rank is 33, with a PDI score of 54. The United States' rank is 38, with a PDI score of 40. These rankings highlight several points: from the American perspective, Japan is a more vertical society; however, Japan is not as hierarchical as the other thirty-two countries. Japan does not have a caste system, although there was a class system during the Edo era (A.D. 1603–1867).

Third, cross-cultural, multidimensional research is a useful tool for implementing culturally sensitive management processes in the global context. For instance, one cross-cultural business alliance between France and the United States experienced various cultural clashes. A key U.S. manager, who slowly but patiently worked through others according to a philosophy of empowerment, was regarded as weak by the French, who were used to a more directive style.[20] Sure enough, France ranks 15/16 (tied with Hong Kong), with a power-distance index score of 68, higher than those of Japan and the United States.[21] No wonder that, from the French employees' view, the American manager looked wimpy. Fons Trompenaars also reported another apt example:[22]

> Many multinational companies apply formulas in overseas areas that are derived from, and are successful in, their own cultures. International management consulting firms of Anglo-Saxon origin are still using similar methods to the neglect of cultural differences.
>
> An Italian computer company received advice from a prominent international management consulting firm to restructure to a matrix organization. It did so and failed; the task-oriented approach of the matrix structure challenged loyalty to the functional boss. In Italy bosses are like fathers, you cannot have two fathers.

This one failure does not mean that no U.S. management concepts, including empowerment and matrix systems, can work in

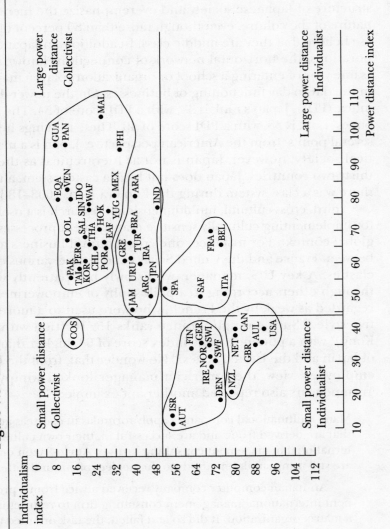

Figure 7.3. Index of Individualism and Power Distance.

Abbreviation	Country or region	Abbreviation	Country or region
ARA	Arab-speaking countries (Egypt, Iraq, Kuwait, Lebanon, Libya, Saudi Arabia, United Arab Emirates)	ISR	Israel
		ITA	Italy
		JAM	Jamaica
		JPN	Japan
		KOR	South Korea
ARG	Argentina	MAL	Malaysia
AUL	Australia	MEX	Mexico
AUT	Austria	NET	Netherlands
BEL	Belgium	NOR	Norway
BRA	Brazil	NZL	New Zealand
CAN	Canada	PAK	Pakistan
CHL	Chile	PAN	Panama
COL	Colombia	PER	Peru
COS	Costa Rica	PHI	Philippines
DEN	Denmark	POR	Portugal
EAF	East Africa (Ethiopia, Kenya, Tanzania, Zambia)	SAF	South Africa
		SAL	Salvador
		SIN	Singapore
EQA	Ecuador	SPA	Spain
FIN	Finland	SWE	Sweden
FRA	France	SWI	Switzerland
GBR	Great Britain	TAI	Taiwan
GER	Germany	THA	Thailand
GRE	Greece	TUR	Turkey
GUA	Guatemala	URU	Uruguay
HOK	Hong Kong	USA	United States
IDO	Indonesia	VEN	Venezuela
IND	India	WAF	West Africa (Ghana, Nigeria, Sierra Leone)
IRA	Iran	YUG	Yugoslavia
IRE	Ireland (Republic of)		

Source: Geert Hofstede, *Cultures and Organizations: Software of the Mind* (Maidenhead, Berkshire, U.K.: McGraw-Hill, 1991), pp. 54–55. Reproduced by permission of Geert Hofstede.

Table 7.1. The United States and Japan in Geert Hofstede's Research.

Rank/Country/Score

Individualism			Power Distance			Uncertainty Avoidance			Masculinity			Long-Term Orientation[a]		
1	USA	91	1	Malaysia	104	1	Greece	112	1	Japan	95	1	China	118
2	Australia	90	2/3	Guatemala	95	2	Portugal	104	2	Austria	79	2	Hong Kong	96
3	UK	89	2/3	Panama	95	3	Guatemala	101	3	Venezuela	73	3	Taiwan	87
												4	Japan	80
22/23	Japan	46	33	Japan	54	7	Japan	92	15	USA	62			
			38	USA	40	43	USA	46				17	USA	29
51	Panama	11	51	Denmark	18	51	Denmark	23	51	Netherlands	14	21	Philippines	19
52	Equador	8	52	Israel	13	52	Jamaica	13	52	Norway	8	22	Nigeria	16
53	Guatemala	6	53	Austria	11	53	Singapore	8	53	Sweden	5	23	Pakistan	00

Source: Adapted from Geert Hofstede, *Cultures and Organizations: Software of the Mind* (Maidenhead, Berkshire, U.K.: McGraw-Hill, 1991).

[a]The number of countries for the long-term-orientation index is 23.

other countries. But rather than assuming that these concepts apply in every situation, managers and consultants must be aware of cultural barriers and take a cautious approach in introducing new systems. For instance, Ciba-Geigy Japan, a subsidiary of the Swiss chemical company, successfully introduced the concept of empowerment to its Japanese employees. Since they realized that *empowerment* is a difficult word to translate into Japanese language, they defined it in this way:[23]

$$Empowerment = Direction \times Autonomy \times Support$$

Direction: managers and employees jointly decide the direction according to employees' level of competency.

Autonomy: give autonomy to front-line employees so that they can make decisions.

Support: managers support employees accordingly to achieve their goals.

If one of the above elements is missing (that is, zero), there is no empowerment. In addition, because of the nature of the multiplier, each employee can adjust the level of direction, autonomy, and support. With such an arrangement, the concept of empowerment was accepted by the Japanese employees.

Applying Cultural Data to Practice: Cultural-Parameter Analysis

The five social and cultural dimensions derived from Hofstede's research play a major role in leadership, motivation, and other management issues. Following are critical differences in organizational practices;[24] managers may use these indicators to form their own corporate styles:

Collectivism	*Individualism*
The employer-employee relationship is perceived in moral terms, like a family link. Management is management of groups.	The employer-employee relationship is a contract based on mutual advantage. Management is management of individuals.

Large Power Distance

Centralization is popular.
Subordinates expect to be
told what to do.

Small Power Distance

Decentralization is popular.
Subordinates expect to be
consulted.

Strong Uncertainty Avoidance

There is caution about new
ideas.
Precision and punctuality
come naturally.
People are motivated by
security and esteem or
belongingness.

Weak Uncertainty Avoidance

There is acceptance of new
ideas.
Precision and punctuality
have to be learned.
People are motivated by
achievement and esteem or
belongingness.

Masculinity

People live in order to work.
Stress is on equity, competition between colleagues,
and performance.

Femininity

People work in order to live.
Stress is on equality, solidarity,
and quality of work life.

Long-Term Orientation

There is perseverance toward
slow results.

Short-Term Orientation

Quick results are expected.

We can use these dimensions in cultural-parameter analysis,
which is a method of analyzing critical issues using cultural quantitative data and qualitative information to help the strategic decision-making process. The following is one example.

A pharmaceutical company had a marketing problem. Four
years ago it had developed a new drug. However, before it began
to sell the drug, some medical journals published the concerns of
several doctors who were worried about its potential side effects.
The company proved that the drug was safe and began to sell it
three years ago in major markets in various countries. Despite its
potentially negative image, the drug sold well in most countries—
except for Japan. Japanese doctors were reluctant to use the drug
because of the initial negative opinions. The company conse-

quently restructured its marketing strategy and function. A joint task force was established, composed of Japanese staff members, U.S. marketing managers, technical support staff, and consultants. In the beginning, the U.S. group and the Japanese group could not agree. The U.S. group would say, "Why is it only in Japan that we can't sell this drug?" The Japanese group would respond, "Japanese doctors still remember the negative press the drug received three years ago. It is just not possible for them to forget."

During the next three months of research and planning, the task force identified some key strategies. One arose from a conversation between the cross-cultural management consultant and the U.S. marketing manager. The consultant asked the manager, "Although you said that you didn't have any problems selling this product in other countries, were there any countries where you encountered similar reactions from the local doctors?" After reviewing the marketing reports for the last three years and holding discussions with managers in Europe and other Asian countries, the U.S. marketing manager replied, "Although we did well in Europe as a whole, in Belgium doctors showed strong resistance to using our drug." This comment caught the attention of the consultant because Belgium is a country of high uncertainty avoidance, scoring even higher than Japan. As a medical product, the drug would naturally be influenced by the uncertainty-avoidance index. It made sense that Belgian doctors would show reactions similar to those of Japanese doctors.

The task force examined the strategies and action plans they had used in Belgium. They reviewed the Belgian promotion tools and learned how the Belgian branch had convinced the doctors. They then adapted the Belgian strategies to the Japanese market. This plan worked well, not only because it transferred the key factors for success into a similar cultural environment, *but also because the company was able to change the Japanese side's perception that Japan was a unique market.* In such ways, we can identify specific cultural parameters that affect particular products and markets and apply them more efficiently both to local and global marketing strategies.

In concluding this chapter, I offer a warning that may sound contradictory. Whenever we encounter any individual or any situation, we have to first abandon what we know and be prepared to adopt a new frame of reference. Tools are important, but we have to be free from the preconceptions that come with them. Tom Peters has written very clearly about this issue:[25]

> "The test of a first-rate intelligence," F. Scott Fitzgerald once wrote, "is the ability to hold two opposed ideas in mind at the same time and still retain the ability to function." So, regarding the issue at hand, can you pass the F. Scott Fitzgerald test? Namely: Can you grasp the notion that creating and leveraging knowledge to create value makes sense while simultaneously embracing the idea that there exists an equally important need to forget what you know?

Chapter Eight

High-Context, High-Content Management

The Direction of Global Organizations

Creativity and adaptation are born of tension, passion and conflict. Contention does more than make us more creative. It makes us whole, it propels us along the journey of development.
RICHARD PASCALE[1]

We have examined cultural differences and have identified the five core competencies and seven mental disciplines that lead to effective transcultural management. As we delve deeper into issues of cultural context, we face the oldest and most demanding management issue today: managing dichotomy. In this chapter we first look at the concept of dichotomy and its place in the global organization and then explore a new paradigm of global business: high-context, high-content management.

Dichotomy and the Global Organization

Percy Barnevik, CEO of ABB, Asea Brown Boveri Ltd., has said, "ABB is an organization with three internal contradictions. We want to be global and local, big and small, radically decentralized with centralized reporting and control."[2] This statement by Barnevik about his organization articulates a point that is also advocated by many leading thinkers, that the cutting edge of management revolves around handling duality and dilemmas. Emerging global work situations constantly challenge us, posing various dilemmas. Paul A. L. Evans and Yves Doz addressed this issue in "Dualities: A Paradigm for Human Resource and Organizational Development in Complex Multinationals":[3]

> The concept of duality appears to lead to an emerging paradigm for management and organization in a world of rapid change and high complexity, a world where global business requires multi-dimensional organizational capabilities. Current management paradigms no longer provide an adequate frame.

Looking back at the evolution of globalization (see Figure 4.1), the international ethnocentric organization has as its assumption, "The home office knows business better than the local office." The multinational polycentric organization has the opposite assumption: "The local office knows the market better than the home office." The truly global organization has to reach a synthesis of these two opposing approaches, which requires global integration and local autonomy. In today's global environment, everyone in the organization has to manage the dichotomy of the home office and the host country. What we have to do is to think globally *and* locally and then act appropriately.[4] It is not too much to say that global business is the management of dichotomy (see Table 8.1).[5]

There are many crucial dualities in cross-cultural work situations; those involving Japan and the United States, as we have noted, include the tendency to be group-oriented or individualistic, vertical or horizontal, and risk-avoiding or risk-taking. Global organizations have to face these dichotomies and benefit from contention. However, as Richard Pascale has noted, contention carries a stigma: managers are uncomfortable with it and it is often misconstrued as a sign of organizational ill health. In reality, not many see contention as an "engine of inquiry," although this is an essential activity if we want to keep our paradigm current.[6] We often hear such statements as "Let's build an organization by taking the best from each culture." However, not many people are aware that "the best" of a culture may itself contain dualities and dilemmas. We have to rethink a question that is eternal in human history, for both the East and the West, and apply it to our current business environment: how to integrate yin and yang, thesis and antithesis.

Table 8.1. Common Dualities in Today's Global Business.

Headquarters	— Local Operation
Customization	— Standardization
Process-oriented	— Result-oriented
Networking	— Hierarchy
Competition	— Partnership
Differentiation	— Integration
Loose	— Tight
Control	— Empowerment
Planned	— Opportunistic
Vision	— Reality
Decentralization	— Centralization
Top-down	— Bottom-up
Tolerance	— Forthrightness
Flexibility	— Focus
Inductive	— Deductive
Individual	— Group-oriented
Horizontal	— Vertical
Specific	— Holistic
Analytical	— Intuitive
Informal	— Formal
Direct	— Indirect
Short-term	— Long-term
Change	— Continuity

In managing dualities, Evans and Doz provide a useful concept, which they call the "zone of complementarity."[7] Most of the qualities of a social system have a corresponding complementary quality, and together they form a duality. If we go beyond the zone of complementarity between two qualities such as "individualistic" and "cooperative," then one of the two values will dominate and will be negatively evaluated ("individualistic" becomes "uncooperative" while "cooperative" becomes "conformist"). We must balance the complementary qualities, whether they are corporate integration and local responsiveness or individualism and teamwork.

The balance between complementary dualities has to be dynamic rather than static[8] in order to respond to changes in the environment. At the same time, if an organization focuses on only one polarity, it creates a state of crisis. The matrix system is a tool that helps organizations to prevent such crises (see Chapter Four). Many global corporations, including those striving to become global, have introduced a matrix system, with, for example, the country manager's focus on local needs on one axis and the product manager's focus on global integration on the other. Merits of matrix organizations include quick information sharing and flexible response through coordination of resources for a client and/or project. The critical drawbacks of matrix organizations lie in their potential for conflict because of dual reporting and authority. In addition, matrix organizations often confuse local employees who have two bosses (for example, a country manager and a product manager). Successful matrix organizations require a clearly defined vision, a system for conflict resolution, and a good understanding of how to manage dilemmas.

In this sense, using a matrix is useful, but not enough, to grasp the essence of managing dilemmas. Charles Hampden-Turner has developed an excellent model that emphasizes the key characteristics of dualities and the principles for managing them. He reconciled the two opposing values of individualism and collectivism by placing them in a cycle that shows the sequence of changing perspectives, as follows:[9]

a. Individualism: Encourage individual freedom and responsibility, however . . .
b. We do not want to degenerate into self-centeredness or forced compromise, so we must . . .
c. Collectivism: Encourage individualism to work for consensus in the interests of the group, although . . .
d. We need to avoid conformism and slow decision-making, so we must . . . [returns to a].

Fons Trompenaars explains the benefits of this model and its cross-cultural implications:[10]

We all go through these cycles, but starting from different points and conceiving of them as means or ends. The individualist culture sees the individual as "the end," and improvements to collective arrangements as the means to achieve it. The collectivist culture sees the group as its end, and improvements to individual capacities as a means to that end. Yet if the relationship is truly circular, the decision to label one element as an end and another as means is arbitrary. By definition, circles never end. Every "end" is also means to another goal. This is closer to my own conviction that individualism finds its fulfillment in service to the group, while group goals are of demonstrable value to individuals only if those individuals are consulted and participate in the process of developing them. The reconciliation is not easy, but possible.

It is crucial for a cross-cultural team to share their common understanding of two different values. Especially when each party sees its own core value as positive and the value of the other party as negative, it is important to show that the two values are not isolated but interrelated.

One Japanese subsidiary of an American company learned mutual values by going through this cycle. A major complaint by Japanese managers concerned the frequent policy changes at U.S. headquarters. On the other hand, to the American managers, the Japanese managers looked too slow. In the beginning, both sides persisted in their own core value and saw the value of the other side as opposing theirs:

The Japanese managers advocated consistency. They said, "We need firmness and stability. Our clients also feel comfortable with our consistency."

The American managers advocated change. They said, "Change is a progress. If we cannot change ourselves, we are dead."

In an attempt to resolve their opposing values, the Japanese and American managers began to reconsider their positions:

The Japanese managers took a second look at consistency. They said, "Our business environment, competitors, and clients are changing. Thus, we need to be flexible and open for change."

The American managers took a second look at change. They said, "We need solid foundations for all of us to make commitments among ourselves and to our clients. Thus, we must value consistency."

At this point, the Japanese and American managers changed to a cycle that led toward reconciliation rather than opposition. Together they developed guiding principles that they decided to use for daily behaviors, as follows:

We value both consistency and change because we know that both create our edge in the industry. Thus, based on our corporate vision and values, we stay quick and flexible in our operations.

A Möbius strip can help us to visualize a new view of duality (Figure 8.1). Drawing a line between two values is the first-dimensional view, because the first dimension constitutes a world of one single line. Drawing a circle on the paper to connect two values is the second-dimensional view, because the second dimension constitutes a world of one flat plane. The Möbius strip provides us with an effective metaphor to shift from the second to the third dimension, which is our living world, made up of the second dimension plus height. Moving into the third dimension, we can break our limitations. In practice, the addition of the new dimension has to be done in the area of our perceptions, frames of reference, and mindsets. Indeed, because dualities reflect mindsets, or ways of thinking,[11] they are only manageable *if we change our mindsets.*

Rethinking the Perception of the Framework

During the last several decades there have been many attempts to integrate American and Japanese management systems and build a synthesized model. Researchers and thinkers have noted the

Figure 8.1. Two Values on a Möbius Strip.

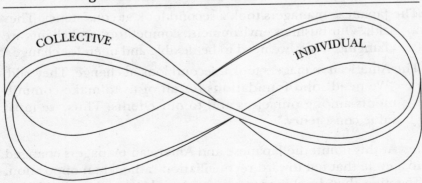

salient differences between the two systems and have tried to synthesize the mostly opposing dualities. For instance, the quality circle, a U.S. system that was introduced to Japan by W. Edwards Deming in 1950, had a "hard" statistical and technical foundation.[12] Japanese companies internalized the quality circle into their organizations and created the concept of the total quality circle,[13] which included such "soft" aspects as employee motivation and empowerment. Some of the Japanese cultural variables, such as group orientation, holistic thinking, long-term planning, and valuing continuity, nourished quality circle activities. The total quality circle was then reimported into the United States and led to the total quality management (TQM) movement. From theory Z to reengineering and time-based competition, many new management frameworks were born because of synergistic management interaction between the United States and Japan.

On the other hand, few of these great management theories actually work in cross-cultural organizations. Not all "synergy models" are applicable in managing dualities and creating synergistic global organizations. Why is it difficult to find organizations that have achieved what the great thinkers described? Lack of understanding of the nature of cross-cultural organizations and of what is needed to manage dualities are no doubt major causes. Also, before questioning a theory we often forget to question the perceptions of the thinkers and managers. If we do, we will find two key perceptual problems; solving these problems calls for deliberate paradigm shifts.

First, for a long time we have been indoctrinated into the old management paradigm that hard (structure and system) can manage soft (culture and people). In other words, hard comes first and soft is secondary. Until recently, managers did not realize the value of the soft skills. Noel Tichy found that from World War II until 1980, many U.S. companies were weak in both the hard skills, such as budget, manufacturing, marketing, distribution, head count, and finances, and the soft skills, such as values, culture, vision, leadership style, and innovative behavior. Then, during the decade of the 1980s, they became stronger at the hard skills. Tichy believes that the long-term challenge is to become stronger at the soft skills, because it is these skills that create the conditions for new products and innovation.[14] Christopher Bartlett and Sumantra Ghoshal use an apt metaphor to convey this shift in perception:[15]

The companies that fell into the organizational trap assumed that changing their formal structure (anatomy) would force changes in interpersonal relationships and decision processes (physiology), which in turn would reshape the individual attitudes and actions of managers (psychology).

Indeed, the companies that are most successful at developing multidimensional organizations begin at the far end of the anatomy-physiology-psychology sequence. Their first objective is to alter the organizational psychology—the broad corporate beliefs and norms that shape managers' perceptions and actions. Then, by enriching and clarifying communication and decision processes, companies reinforce these psychological changes with improvements in organizational physiology. Only later do they consolidate and confirm their progress by realigning organizational anatomy through changes in the formal structure.

Figure 8.2 illustrates the first paradigm shift that we have to make to build a synthesized model for transcultural management. The new paradigm works through culture and process to achieve a new structure. We are seeing a similar shift almost everywhere.

Figure 8.2. Managing Priority: From the Old to the New Paradigm.

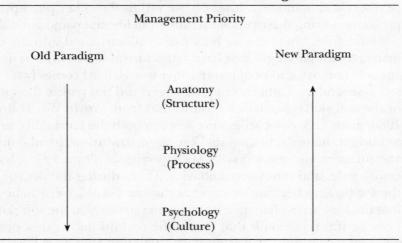

Management Priority

Old Paradigm		New Paradigm
	Anatomy (Structure)	
	Physiology (Process)	
	Psychology (Culture)	

Source: Adapted from Christopher Bartlett and Sumantra Ghoshal, "Matrix Management: Not a Structure, a Frame of Mind," *Harvard Business Review,* July–August 1990, p. 140.

According to Fritjof Capra, the internationally known physicist, we are facing a crisis of perception, and what we need is to shift our perception from the old paradigm (the view of the universe as a mechanical system composed of elementary building blocks and, correspondingly, the view of the human body as a machine) to the new paradigm (a holistic worldview, seeing the world as an integrated whole rather than a dissociated collection of parts).[16]

Deepak Chopra, who combines quantum physics theory and Ayurveda (India's ancient healing tradition), observes that "consciousness conceives, constructs, governs, and becomes the physical body."[17] This view holds a key message for business thinkers and practitioners about the importance of intention. In fact, Gary Hamel and C. K. Prahalad advocate the value of strategic intent, ambition out of proportion to a company's resources (which they identified through their research on companies that have been global leaders over the past twenty years), as the guiding principle for creating global leadership in corporations.[18] They caution that the application of conventional concepts such as "strategic fit" (between resources and opportunities), "generic strategies" (low cost versus differentiation versus focus), and the "strategy hierarchy" (goals, strategies, and tactics) have often abetted the process of competitive decline.[19] Interestingly enough, these conventional concepts are related to a view of society as a competitive struggle for existence, which Capra named as part of the old paradigm inherited from the social Darwinists.[20] It is true that systems and structure can eventually influence intent. However, the basic principle is that systems and structure follow intent, not the other way around.

For example, an American company introduced a matrix system to its Japan branch office: one axis representing marketing function and the other representing research function. This new matrix system confused Japanese managers because of the potential drawbacks of the organizational system. Some managers believed that the concept of the matrix system was developed by the American company, not knowing that it is one option for organizational structures. The staff in the Japan branch focused on the systems and the structure, such as the chain of command. Once the intent of the matrix system (to establish customer-driven product development) was clarified and this intent was translated into their own language, the matrix system started working in the Japan branch.

The second paradigm shift that we have to make goes even deeper. Whether we say that soft creates hard or combine the two aspects, there is still a sense of separation between soft and hard skills. This sense of segregation also creates a polarity between soft experts and hard experts. For instance, as Noel Tichy pointed out, traditional training in soft skills focuses on cross-cultural awareness, interpersonal skills, and team activities, but it is devoid of hard-skills content.[21] The new paradigm is a holistic view that sees soft in hard and hard in soft, as shown in Figure 8.3. According to Michael Ray and Rochelle Myers, the crucial point of this yin-yang model is that "the white dot in the black and the black in the white suggest the always present potential for change and creation."[22]

As we saw in the previous chapter, the terms *context* and *content* can help to clarify our perception of reshaping soft and hard skills. The major traits of context and content are as follows:

Figure 8.3. Hard or Soft: From the Old to the New Paradigm.

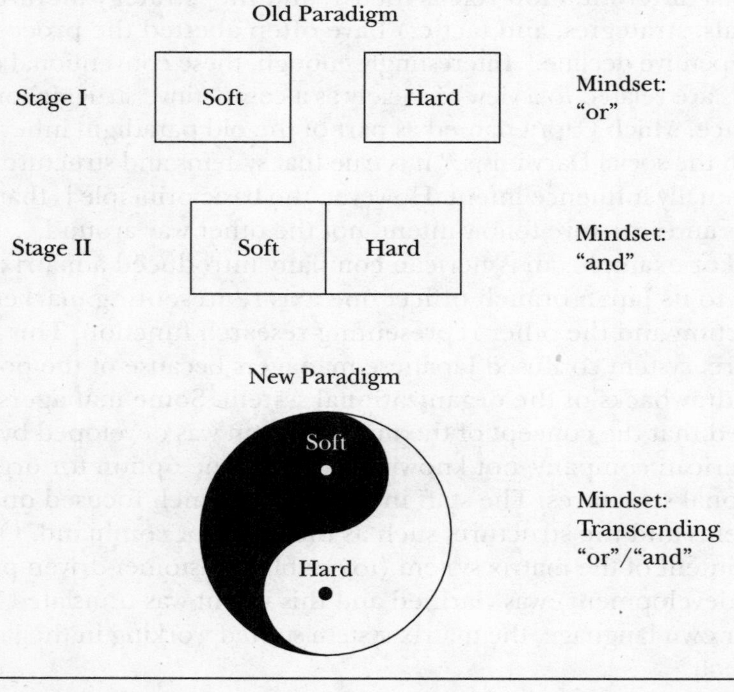

Old Paradigm

Stage I   Soft   Hard   Mindset: "or"

Stage II   Soft | Hard   Mindset: "and"

New Paradigm

Soft
Hard   Mindset: Transcending "or"/"and"

Context	*Content*
Implicit	Explicit
Intuitive	Analytical
Qualitative	Quantitative
Invisible	Visible
Intangible	Tangible
Transdimensional	Two- or three-dimensional
Analog	Digital
Yin	Yang

For instance, intuitive insight is a context skill, whereas analytical ability is a content skill. Content strategy includes traditional strength, weakness, opportunity, and threat (SWOT) analysis and strategic fit based on hard data, while context strategy focuses on corporate culture and the invisible interaction between members of the organization. However, U.S. management experts often underestimate contextual issues because of their high-content, low-context management approach. This is reflected in their communication style. They can easily see content but not context. Pascale points out why many companies cannot implement many of the new management concepts:[23]

> To be sure, there are valid aspects to most of these ideas. What's wrong is that, overwhelmingly, companies apply them in a piecemeal fashion and shift from one to another too frequently. What is lacking is a grasp of the larger context in which they must be embedded.

The larger context includes the cultural context—both national and organizational. As we have seen when looking at institutionalized cross-cultural impediments, U.S. management thinkers and practitioners seldom realize their underlying assumptions (that is, their belief that organizations can be changed from the top down and that national cultural differences are not important). No wonder, then, that many American companies that rushed to copy Japanese systems such as quality circles and just-in-time deliveries were hampered by cultural differences.[24] It is not feasible to introduce the visible content of the just-in-time delivery system without considering the context of the Japanese vender-customer relationship in which it developed.

Not only American companies but also Japanese companies make mistakes when applying management concepts across cultures. Historically, Japanese companies have been good at introducing some American management systems and modifying them to fit their system. However, high-context Japanese managers cannot always correctly read the context of these American management theories. They have to understand that the United States has a different context from that of Japan. For instance, although reengineering became fashionable in Japan as *reenjiniaring,* there was a lot of confusion with *ristra* (restructuring). Whenever American management buzzwords are transcribed into *Katakana* (one of the two phonetic scripts for Japanese writing, especially used for foreign words), the original meaning and context tend to be left out of the concept. This lack of understanding of the larger context causes a discrepancy between the conceptual framework and its practice in both Japan and the United States. In order to minimize this gap, those who introduce new concepts to their organizations have to shift their perceptions.

High-Context, High-Content Management: A New Paradigm of Global Business

Marilyn Ferguson tells us the need of perceptual shift: "Context of work is as important as content—not just what you do but *how* you do it."[25] As we have seen in Chapter Seven, U.S. management style can be characterized as high-content, while Japanese management style is high-context. The main focus of high-content management is content—something tangible, visible, and quantitatively measurable, such as product specifications and cash-flow statements. On the other hand, high-context management values context—something intangible, invisible, and more qualitative, such as organizational culture and corporate visions. High-context, high-content (HCHC) management is not simply the sum of the two styles. It requires a drastic shift in our perception of context and content. The terms *content* and *context* cover a wide range of variables, as well as the various dimensions of dilemma and duality that need to be understood and dealt with in global organizations. HCHC management synergizes context and content by allowing the convergence and transformation of soft and hard skills (Figure 8.4). The combination of the HCHC management style, the five core competencies, and the seven mental disciplines provides the direction for the truly global geocentric corporation (Figure 8.5). At the same time, HCHC management provides crucial guidelines for top management, middle managers, staff members, and consultants—guidelines that range from daily operational issues to comprehensive corporate strategic issues.

Compared with the drawbacks of past theories that have tried to synthesize dualities and form a synergistic management model, HCHC management has at least three distinctive features. First, it emphasizes the most fundamental management behavior: communication. Cross-cultural communication skills, one of the five core competencies, are the key to the practice of HCHC management. Second, it stresses cross-cultural durability. Some concepts do not work across cultures. On the other hand, the concept of HCHC

Figure 8.4. Direction of High-Context, High-Content Management.

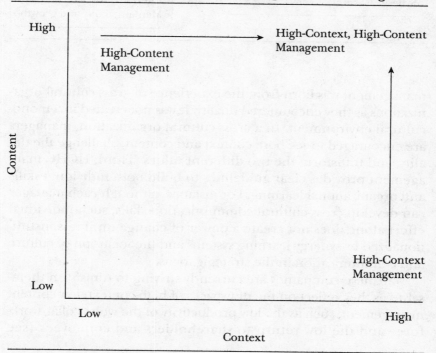

Figure 8.5. Framework of High-Context, High-Content Management.

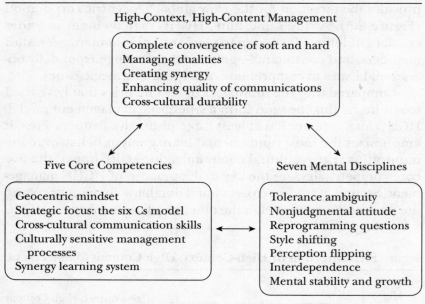

High-Context, High-Content Management

Complete convergence of soft and hard
Managing dualities
Creating synergy
Enhancing quality of communications
Cross-cultural durability

Five Core Competencies

Geocentric mindset
Strategic focus: the six Cs model
Cross-cultural communication skills
Culturally sensitive management
  processes
Synergy learning system

Seven Mental Disciplines

Tolerance ambiguity
Nonjudgmental attitude
Reprogramming questions
Style shifting
Perception flipping
Interdependence
Mental stability and growth

management was born from the experience of cross-cultural organizations as they encountered duality. It was not created in a monocultural environment. In a cross-cultural organization, managers are encouraged to see both context and content, challenge the duality, and transform the two different values. Third, HCHC management provides clear guidelines to build both individual skills and organizational learning. For instance, although each manager can develop cross-cultural communication skills, such individual effort alone does not create a power of change until it is institutionalized by synergy learning systems and the inclusion of culture and communication in the strategic focus.

Japanese companies are currently striving to transform themselves as they reflect on the drawbacks of high-context, low-content management, such as the low productivity of the white-collar workforce and the low return to shareholders and employees (see

Chapter Eleven). Concomitantly, American companies have begun to shift dramatically from low- to high-context management, and many business schools are changing their courses and placing more emphasis on soft skills.[26] There is no doubt that HCHC management is now the direction for both the United States and Japan. Excellent frameworks are emerging that share the common features of HCHC management—one from Japan and one from the United States.

From Japan: The Knowledge-Creating Company

In Japan, Ikujiro Nonaka, a professor at Hitotsubashi University in Tokyo, wrote in the editor's note of the Japanese translation of *Reengineering the Corporation* that one of the key lessons for Japanese businesspeople about reengineering is the importance of converting tacit knowledge about behaviors and management systems into language.[27] The process of converting tacit knowledge into explicit knowledge is at the heart of what he calls "the knowledge-creating company."

According to Nonaka, the knowledge-creating company constantly creates new knowledge, disseminates it widely throughout the organization, and quickly embodies it in new technologies and products.[28] He also emphasizes the importance of the dynamic interaction between two opposing concepts at all levels, such as tacit knowledge and explicit knowledge, the individual and the organization, networks and hierarchy, or bottom-up and top-down management.[29] From his explanation, it is clear that tacit knowledge is the same as context, while explicit knowledge is content: "Tacit knowledge is highly personal. It is hard to formalize and, therefore, difficult to communicate to others."[30] It is "also deeply rooted in action and in an individual's commitment to a specific context."[31] On the other hand, "explicit knowledge is formal and systematic. For this reason, it can be easily communicated and shared, in product specifications or scientific formula or a computer program."[32]

In the knowledge-creating company, the following four patterns of interaction between tacit knowledge and explicit knowledge create a kind of spiral of knowledge:[33]

1. *From tacit to tacit (socialization):* As the apprentice learns the master's skills, one individual shares tacit knowledge directly with another by working closely with him or her. As this is a personalized form of knowledge creation, it cannot easily be leveraged by the organization as a whole. For example, the members of a product development team in the bread-making department of Matsushita Electric Industrial Company volunteered to apprentice themselves to the head baker of the Osaka International Hotel for one year to learn the secret of making tasty bread.

2. *From tacit to explicit (articulation):* When a person is able to articulate her or his tacit knowledge, it is converted into explicit knowledge. As new explicit knowledge, it can be shared throughout an organization. For example, a company controller using the tacit knowledge she has developed during her years on the job created an innovative budget control system.

3. *From explicit to explicit (combination):* An individual can also combine discrete pieces of explicit knowledge into a new whole. This process standardizes and embodies existing knowledge. However, it does not really create new knowledge. Formal education and training at business schools usually take this form.

4. *From explicit to tacit (internalization):* As new explicit knowledge is shared throughout an organization, other employees begin to internalize it—that is, they use it to broaden, extend, and reframe their own tacit knowledge. Internalization is closely related to "learning by doing," including role playing and simulation exercises.

According to Nonaka, "Articulation (converting tacit knowledge into explicit knowledge) and internalization (using that explicit knowledge to extend one's own tacit knowledge base) are the critical steps in this spiral of knowledge." He especially stresses the step of converting tacit knowledge into explicit knowledge: "Indeed, because tacit knowledge includes mental models and beliefs in addition to know-how, moving from the tacit to the explicit is really a process of articulating one's vision of the world—what it is and what it ought to be. . . . To convert tacit knowledge into explicit knowledge means finding a way to express the inexpressible."[34]

The knowledge-creating company embodies an important aspect of HCHC management: the dynamic interaction of context and content. Articulation equals "contentualization," the process of converting context into content, which is indispensable in HCHC management. More than thirty years ago, one of the trailblazers of cross-cultural communication theory, Basil Bernstein, described how different social structures may generate different speech systems or linguistic codes. He characterized the two general coding systems as *restricted code* and *elaborated code*,[35] found in high-context and low-context cultures, respectively. His explanation provides an interesting insight into contentualization:[36]

> In the case of a restricted code, what is transmitted verbally refers to the other person in terms of his status or local group membership. What is said reflects the form of the social relation and its basis of shared assumptions. Speakers using a restricted code are dependent upon these assumptions. The mutually held range of identifications defines the area of common intent and so the range of the code. The dependency underpinning the social relation generating an elaborated code is not of this order. With an elaborated code, the listener is dependent upon the verbal elaboration of meaning. In restricted codes, to varying degrees, the extraverbal channels become objects of special perceptual activity; in elaborated codes it is the verbal channel.

By knowing the nature of these two coding systems, each individual in the knowledge-creating company should become skillful in contentualization, through which he or she can decode context and encode it into content. In this way, the shared assumptions and tacit knowledge that one group holds can be transmitted to other groups and shared throughout the organization. As we saw in the example earlier in this chapter of the American company that introduced a matrix system to its Japanese subsidiary, in a cross-cultural organization it is important to recognize that different individuals and groups may have their own assumptions (in this case, the assumption that everyone was familiar with the concept of a matrix system) that are not always shared throughout the organization.

In order for knowledge transfer to occur between two individuals or organizations, they also have to develop the ability to learn from tacit knowledge and context. This *contextual literacy* is necessary for the contentualization process. An understanding of differences in communication styles and acute observation can help in developing contextual literacy. When a high-context individual (such as a Japanese) develops an ability for contentualization, and a low-context individual (such as an American) develops contextual literacy in the organization, the organization can enhance the dynamic interaction of HCHC management.

Although Nonaka noted that Japanese companies are good at developing the process of exchanging tacit and explicit knowledge, we have to remember that *they are good at it in their own cultural context*. They also need to be able to be good at it in different cultural contexts. In *Ibunka Interface Keiei* ("Intercultural Management"), Kichiro Hayashi wrote about the importance of understanding the Japanese "analog" and the American "digital" styles of learning.[37] He pointed out that traditional Oriental learning systems, such as Zen, are based on analog training systems, with limited verbal explanations and learning through specific behaviors and forms.[38] Japanese managers may think that they don't have to provide digital-style explanations to non-Japanese employees. But they have to realize that their analog learning style is deeply ingrained in their high-context culture and communication style. By doing this and overcoming the cultural context gap between the tacit knowledge holder and the learner, the knowledge-creating company can work effectively across cultures.

From the United States: The Learning Organization

Just as Nonaka made a remarkable contribution to our understanding by decoding the contextual dynamics of organizational learning processes in Japanese companies and encoding them into the content of the knowledge-creating company, so Peter Senge did an equally important job by articulating the intricacy of organizational learning in American companies and converting it into an explicit model as the "learning organization." Senge defined learning organizations as places where people continually expand their capacity to create the results they truly desire, where new and

expansive patterns of thinking are nurtured, where collective as-
piration is set free, and where people are continually learning how
to learn together.

The concept of the learning organization poses a challenge for
those who are not familiar with systems thinking and a holistic way
of seeing the world. Senge's model, which focuses on vital soft
issues such as mental models, team learning processes, and the
underlying assumptions that each individual holds, may sound
completely foreign to low-context, high-content managers who are
not used to seeing soft context.

One of the most significant aspects of Senge's work is the clear
linkage of soft issues and hard corporate management issues. However, some do not appreciate this new perspective. "The learning
organization is so radical that many human resources people (as
well as others) feel uncomfortable with it. They say it's too soft; too
amorphous."[39] This comment led me to remember when I taught a
martial arts class. It was difficult for students to grasp the importance of the spiritual and mental aspects. Some young students
who liked only punching and kicking were skeptical about meditation and breathing exercises. In contrast to the stereotypes of
Japanese martial arts practice, in which the individual meditates
patiently, much like a Zen monk, they did not like "spiritual" training. They did not see martial arts as a holistic discipline and failed
to understand the connection between doing meditation and practicing kicking.

In my teaching, I didn't want to give a mystified explanation
of the spiritual aspect. Instead, I tried to explain things logically
by showing a clear connection between hard and soft techniques.
I said, "We want to become strong and not be defeated by our opponent. In order to handle any attack from our opponent, we
have to sharpen our senses. To do so, we have to be able to read
the other's breathing and not let our opponent read our breath.
But to do this, we have to maintain our mental stability, because
breathing reflects our mental condition. Our minds should not
be occupied with any particular thought or preoccupation. Thus
the stage of *mu* (nothingness) is often said to be important in Zen
philosophy. We meditate in order to reach this stage." In short, we
do soft or spiritual practices in order to achieve a hard result (to
be strong).

The learning organization can enhance its learning opportunities and enrich all aspects of cross-cultural situations. Cross-cultural interfaces provide the optimal opportunity to learn about our underlying assumptions, making us question what we take for granted. Senge wrote:[40]

> Reality is made up of circles but we see straight lines. Herein lie the beginnings of our limitation as system thinkers. One of the reasons for this fragmentation in our thinking stems from our language. Language shapes perception. What we see depends on what we are prepared to see. Western languages, with their subject-verb-object structure, are biased toward a linear view. If we want to see system wide interrelationships, we need a language of interrelationships, a language made up of circles. Without such a language, our habitual ways of seeing the world produce fragmented views and counter-productive actions. . . . Such a language is important in facing dynamically complex issues and strategic choices, especially when individuals, teams and organizations need to see beyond events and into the forces that shape change.

When an organization moves toward becoming a global company and its people experience different kinds of interactions from those in the familiar domestic operation, they inevitably face critically important learning opportunities. These unknown situations should be taken as learning opportunities, not as obstacles. They help us to experience critical changes in our mental models—deeply ingrained assumptions about how we think and how we understand. The best way to have such an experience is to learn a foreign language that is significantly different in terms of its cultural context (for example, if you are a native English speaker, try to learn Japanese or Indonesian). You will develop an awareness of your own thought patterns.

The concept of the learning organization has a high potential for cross-cultural durability because of its holistic structure and its deep insights into metalevel (unconscious-level) human interactions. However, its success depends on the ability of those who actually introduce the concept to overseas practitioners, implement the program, and facilitate the team. The learning organization is not a trend but a way people think about learning, relate to each other, and connect to their organization.[41] Likewise, HCHC management is the way people think, act, and work effectively across cultures. Both transform the workplace into a *dojo* (literally a place of Tao, used in martial arts and Zen, a place for both physical and spiritual training), where we learn and practice disciplines and enrich ourselves. Indeed, "until people can make their 'work space' a learning space, learning will always be a 'nice idea'— peripheral, not central."[42] The highly respected karate master, Gichin Funakoshi, who first introduced karate from Okinawa to the Japanese mainland, wrote: "Some youthful enthusiasts of karate believe that it can be learned only from instructors in a *dojo*, but such men are mere technicians, not true *karateka*. There is a Buddhist saying that 'any place can be a *dojo*,' and that is a saying that anyone who wants to follow the way of karate must never forget."[43]

Part Three

The United States and Japan

Chapter Nine

Root Causes of Cross-Cultural Business Conflict

*In short, the Swedes will become more Swedish, the
Chinese, more Chinese. And the French, God help us,
more French.*
JOHN NAISBITT[1]

The following three chapters address specific situations found in
the U.S.–Japan cross-cultural business environment: American
companies in Japan, Japanese companies in the United States, and
strategic alliances between the two countries. As we know, there
are distinct cultural differences between the two countries, and examining the cross-cultural business environment of each provides
us with an insight into managing across cultures in a global context. In this chapter we focus on the root causes of cross-cultural
business conflict and the issues that are common to both Japanese
and American organizations.

Analyzing the Cross-Cultural Business Environment

As noted in the preface to this book, there are two critical gaps in
the U.S.–Japan cross-cultural business environment:

1. *A gap in the flow of information:* American managers are more
   outspoken than their Japanese employees concerning the issues

American companies have in Japan; on the other hand, American employees are much more outspoken than their Japanese managers concerning the issues Japanese companies have in the United States. Consequently, the flow of information in the cross-cultural business environment is often unbalanced.

2. *A cross-cultural communication gap:* A communication gap occurs between American researchers and Japanese employees. Japanese employees are frequently accused of failing to provide feedback, and American researchers may not be aware of the cultural variables and differences in communication styles.

Those who have worked on one side of the equation (Japanese companies in the United States or American companies in Japan) sometimes fail to see the issues from the other side. For instance, an article by John E. Rehfeld in the *Harvard Business Review,* "What Working for a Japanese Company Taught Me," provides an insider's viewpoint on what it is like to work for a Japanese company. One statement, however, indicates that the author has forgotten the other point of view. He writes, "Another frustration for Americans is the Japanese insistence on quantifying everything, even intangible things."[2] I have heard the same comment again and again from Japanese employees, who complain that American managers constantly demand quantitative data. I have also heard the comment from Japanese managers working for Japanese companies and American managers working for American companies. It seems to be a common complaint no matter what the culture is. In cross-cultural situations, this type of frustration seems to frequently give rise to such judgments, as the Japanese do not completely trust individual personal judgments, especially when they come from *gaijin*[3] (outsiders), and American managers do not completely trust *nihonjin* (Japanese) managers in American companies in Japan.

People tend to be more apprehensive about questions of trust when they arise across cultures than when they occur in a domestic environment. In order to analyze cross-cultural business issues adequately, it is important to clarify the common problems and identify the specific issues on each side of the equation. As Figure 9.1 indicates, the United States and Japan share some issues and problems.

Figure 9.1. U.S.–Japan Cross-Cultural Management Issues.

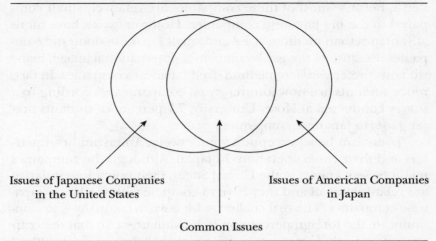

Issues of Japanese Companies
in the United States

Issues of American Companies
in Japan

Common Issues

Common Issues in the Cross-Cultural Business Environment

Gaishi (foreign-capital companies in Japan) are a popular topic in cross-cultural business circles, and much has been written about them by American scholars, former expatriates, and consultants. One of the most discussed "problems" in *gaishi* is the issue of recruiting Japanese managers and employees. I have often been asked by American managers who have read about *gaishi* employment issues whether it is true that they can get only second-class citizens for their Japanese operations. My response is that it depends on the size of the organization, its history in the Japanese market, the nature of the product, and name recognition.

It is true that *gaishi* companies have more difficulty recruiting employees than do major Japanese companies. However, Japanese medium-sized and small companies also face the same challenge. There are nearly two million companies in Japan. Of these, about thirteen hundred companies, called *ichibu jyo-jyo kaisha* (listed on the Tokyo, Osaka, and Nagoya stock exchanges, section I), capture most of the top-notch college graduates. It is not easy for the approximately fifteen hundred *gaishi* companies to hire the top students, because most of these companies are relatively small compared to the big Japanese companies. However, *gaishi* have more advantages than medium-sized and small Japanese domestic companies. Because of the *gaishi* companies' international image, many students prefer *gaishi* to medium-sized Japanese companies. In fact, more students are now joining *gaishi* companies. According to a survey conducted at Hosei University, 7.7 percent of students prefer *gaishi* to Japanese companies.[4]

There can be a perception gap between American headquarters and their *gaishi* operations in Japan. Although the companies might be well known in the United States, their operations in Japan are relatively small and they have to compete with the larger Japanese companies. The real challenge for a *gaishi* company is to communicate the foreign perception to headquarters, so that they can strategize jointly. In order to see the real challenge of cross-cultural business issues, we have to compare American companies in Japan with Japanese companies in Japan, and Japanese companies in the United States with American companies in the United States (Figure 9.2). Such a comparison helps us to avoid a one-dimensional, shortsighted argument and to identify the structural cross-cultural management issues that repeatedly occur regardless of the nature of the business.

Keeping in mind the above framework of overlapping issues, let's examine some of the common areas of complaints mentioned by local employees from both cultures.

> *"The rotation cycle of expatriate managers is too short. They can't do a good job in such a short period."*

In most cases, the length of an assignment is three years, although the trend now is to shorten assignments from three years to one year.[5] For top management positions in subsidiaries, the length of an assignment is sometimes five years. Few assignees stay for ten years. However, the length of the assignment is not always an issue. If the assignee can build a good relationship with the local employees and make a recognizable contribution, we may not hear this kind of comment from the local employees.

Figure 9.2. Another View of
U.S.–Japan Cross-Cultural Management Issues.

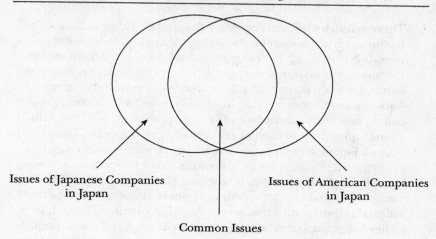

Issues of Japanese Companies
in Japan

Issues of American Companies
in Japan

Common Issues

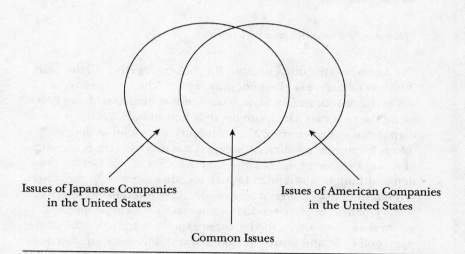

Issues of Japanese Companies
in the United States

Issues of American Companies
in the United States

Common Issues

"There is a glass ceiling in this company. If you want to be promoted, you have to speak their language."

There is much criticism regarding the so-called glass ceiling in Japanese corporations and the lack of delegation to local executives. It is true that Japanese companies lag behind American and European multinational corporations in terms of developing multicultural management teams. However, it is also true that many Japanese employees working for *gaishi* encounter this same glass ceiling and an apparent lack of career opportunities. Those who cannot speak English well often comment on this issue. Thus, although Japanese companies in the United States are often criticized for their glass ceilings, it is shortsighted to promote a "them against us" perception that is based simply on the percentage of foreign national executives without considering the language and cultural infrastructure that we examined in Chapter Three. It is easier for *gaishi* to hire a Japanese who can read and speak English than for *nikkei kigyo* (Japanese companies in the United States) to hire an American who can read and speak Japanese.

"They live in a nice area and stick together."

The Japanese are quite infamous for sticking together all the time. But this characteristic does not only apply to the Japanese. When I was at the American Graduate School of International Management, the program had approximately four hundred foreign students from sixty countries. Many students spent a lot of time with others from their country. Although it was easy to identify a group of Asians because of the color of their hair, French or German students, although they tended to stick together as much as the other foreign students, could not be so easily recognized from a distance. Many Japanese expatriates do not interact with local people and spend their time within the Japanese expatriate triangle (the company, golf club, and Japanese food market), but there are also quite a few American expatriates who do not venture from their triangle (the company, the Tokyo American Club, and their condominium in Roppongi). Such facilities may help in providing a taste of home and in assisting assignees with culture shock. Unfortunately, however, some expatriates have limited exposure to the local culture yet consider themselves experts on it after returning home.

"They are always looking toward headquarters, not to us and our customers."

This is a common complaint from employees in both countries. Assignees have to stay in touch with their headquarters. This fact in itself is not an issue. However, it does become a problem if the expatriate is constantly concerned about headquarters and does not concentrate enough on the local assignment. It is natural for expatriates to have these concerns because in most cases they are involved in a tug-of-war between headquarters and the local operation.

Behind the above complaints is a sense of distrust, resentment, and negative feelings toward others that is produced by cross-cultural mismanagement, both at the organizational level and in individual interactions. Managing this negative energy is a major challenge for any organization that is striving to become a global company. The key to managing these concerns lies in how well organizations can implement transcultural management and the five core competencies and become truly global corporations, providing support systems for expatriates rather than tearing them in two. For instance, consider the following actions:

- Minimize the psychological distance between headquarters and the local operation by fostering a *geocentric mindset* (for example, personnel exchange and a joint performance review by headquarters and the local staff members). A 360-degree performance appraisal, a method that includes as performance reviewers bosses, colleagues, subordinates, task force members, and outside stakeholders such as suppliers and customers, is becoming popular among American companies. Invite local managers and subordinates as performance reviewers.
- Improve the quality of communication and decrease the information gap between headquarters and the local operation by *cross-cultural communication skills*. Make cross-cultural communication training programs mandatory for everyone who handles cross-cultural interactions.

- Get top management involved with any global learning opportunities to demonstrate *the strategic focus of the six Cs model.* Invite former expatriates to a global workshop (see Chapter Five) to share their experiences.
- Increase knowledge sharing during the regular business meeting by utilizing *synergy learning systems.* Assign cross-cultural process facilitators and continually check the level of communication and understanding during meetings.
- Sensitize everyone to the process of developing a strategy and business plans from cross-cultural perspectives (a *culturally sensitive management process*). Apply structured brainstorming techniques. Do not let the English language dominate the business-planning session. Use controlled side talk effectively (see Chapter Five).

The Nature of Cross-Cultural Organizations

Instituting an evolving human resources system is important but not enough to solve cross-cultural problems. The real challenge is to transform the mindset of each employee in the organization. For instance, simply prolonging the length of an assignment from three years to five or seven years will not change a negative situation if the assignee and local staff members cannot build trust. Unless we focus on these root causes, we merely provide stopgap measures that fail to solve the real problems. In order to uncover these real problems, it is important for us to know the nature of cross-cultural organizations.

Organizations on Either Side of the Bell Curve

In my work with many U.S.–Japan cross-cultural organizations, I have often seen a tendency toward polarization at one end of the spectrum or the other, either positive or negative, dynamic or stagnant, fast-growing or collapsing. Some companies can nurture a sense of trust between the Japanese and American contingents, building a synthesized organization by creating cultural synergy. Others cannot overcome the distrust caused by cultural clashes, which often results in low productivity. This polarization represents much more than simple success or failure, as it would in domestic companies. Yoshihiro Tsurumi, who has been critical of Japanese multi-national companies, observed that Japanese companies in the United States tend to split on either side of a bell curve, with one end consisting of highly effective groups and the other end consisting of highly ineffective groups.[6]

A model of group effectiveness researched by Carol Kovich at the Graduate School of Management, University of California at Los Angeles, which compared small heterogeneous and homogeneous teams, clearly explains this polarization[7] (Figure 9.3). According to Kovich's study, homogeneous groups tend to stay in the middle of a bell curve showing group effectiveness, whereas heterogeneous groups tend to be positioned on either side of the curve, either highly effective or highly ineffective.

Nancy Adler believes that the issue is whether we handle cultural diversity as a valuable resource or as a managerial hindrance. She offers the following message:[8]

Figure 9.3. Cross-Cultural Group Effectiveness.

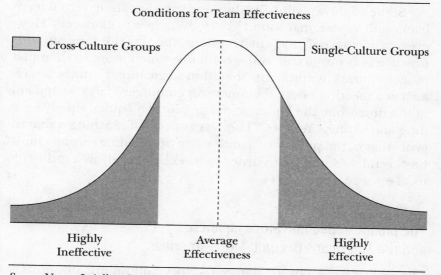

Conditions for Team Effectiveness

Cross-Culture Groups   Single-Culture Groups

Highly   Average   Highly
Ineffective   Effectiveness   Effective

Source: Nancy J. Adler, *International Dimensions of Organizational Behavior* (Boston: Kent, 1991), p. 135. Based on research by Carol Kovach conducted at the Graduate School of Management, University of California at Los Angeles.

Highly productive and less productive teams differ in how they manage their diversity, not, as is commonly believed, in the presence or absence of diversity. When well managed, diversity becomes a productive resource to the team. When ignored, diversity causes process problems that diminish the team's productivity. Since diversity is more frequently ignored than managed, culturally diverse teams often perform below expectations and below the organization's norms.

Adler listed the key factors that enable managers to lead multicultural groups effectively:[9]

- Differences are recognized rather than ignored.
- Members are selected for task-related abilities rather than for ethnicity.
- There is mutual respect rather than ethnocentrism.
- There is equal power rather than cultural dominance.
- There is a superordinate goal rather than individual goals.
- External feedback is given to individuals and the group as a whole.

Some of those points, including shared goals, external feedback, and respect, may sound like nothing new to managers. However, in a cross-cultural environment, the way they are put into practice is as important as the content—much more so than in a monocultural environment. Shared strategic intent cannot be created at a meeting where the American contingent talks 90 percent of the time while the Japanese contingent stays quiet, simply nodding and saying, "Yes, yes." The very process of reaching a shared goal (that is, the process of a joint strategic-planning session) must be carefully examined in order to work effectively in a multicultural environment.

The Japanese Become More Japanese and the Americans Become More American

The second aspect of the nature of cross-cultural organizations is that people tend to persist in their own ways more than they do in a monocultural environment. In other words, Americans become even more impatient with Japanese when they work directly with them, and Japanese become even more defensive toward Americans. A survey of American and French companies by André Lauren shows this kind of polarization. He found cultural differences to be more pronounced among foreign employees working within the same multinational corporation than among employees working for companies in their native countries. This tendency was obvious, especially in attitudes toward conflict management and manager-subordinate relationships (Figure 9.4).[10] This finding counters the general assumption that working together with different nationals in the same multinational corporation will automatically diminish national cultural differences.

We cannot ignore the natural tendency to retrench. Just as we see the French becoming more French, we see the Japanese becoming more Japanese and the Americans becoming more American. Cultural synergy in organizations is not born automatically. It is learned and created through individual commitment and organizational support—through synergy learning systems and the other four competencies.

Best Practice or Worst Practice

One last point when considering the nature of cross-cultural organizations is that quite often people tend to use cultural differences as an excuse not to make an effort to collaborate with each other and improve a situation. Furthermore, people take advantage of their stereotypes of others. For instance, one American manager, believing that the Japanese never complain to their seniors, began to ask his Japanese subordinate to do extra tasks for him. He would not have asked an American subordinate to perform extra tasks, knowing that the subordinate would immediately speak his mind and complain to supervisors. He was taking advantage of the "obedient" stereotype of the Japanese. On the other hand, a Japanese manager harshly criticized his American subordinates, believing that it was constructive criticism and that the Americans would accept his confrontational approach. Such behaviors combine the worst aspects of both nationalities. It is easy to describe methods of creating a synthesized organization by behavioral benchmarking, but it is hard to put them into practice.

Figure 9.4. Enhancement of
Cultural Traits by Cross-Cultural Teams.

"It is important for a manager to have at hand precise answers to most of the questions that his subordinates may raise about their work."

	Multicompany Sample	Single Multinational Corporation (American managers working with French people and French managers working with American people)
U.S.	18%	8%
France	53%	77%

"Most organizations would be better off if conflict could be eliminated forever."

	Multicompany Sample	Single Multinational Corporation Sample
U.S.	6%	4%
France	24%	46%

"Most managers seem to be more motivated by obtaining power than by achieving objectives."

	Multicompany Sample	Single Multinational Corporation Sample
U.S.	36%	12%
France	56%	38%

"Most managers have a clear notion of what we call an organizational structure."

	Multicompany Sample	Single Multinational Corporation Sample
U.S.	52%	85%
France	32%	46%

Source: Adapted from André Laurent, INSEAD, Fontainbleau, France, 1981, in Nancy J. Adler, *International Dimensions of Organizational Behavior* (Boston: Kent, 1991).

Instead, it is much easier to achieve the worst practice by adopting the negative aspects of both nationalities.

Given the nature of cross-cultural organizations, we realize that it is not easy to build a synergistic organization. This awareness itself is a crucial first step in building such an organization. The next key step is to approach the process carefully, with patience. In addition, when encountering problems, view them objectively rather than personally. Many cross-cultural teams experience perceptual shift when they realize that they are not the ones who are in trouble. Once teams and individuals begin to collaborate to solve the problems, they also begin to transcend cultural barriers.

Now that we have covered a few common cross-cultural issues, we will examine some specific situations in the next three chapters, starting with the experience of American companies in Japan.

Chapter Ten

American Companies in Japan

*A Japan strategy is required, and is difficult to put in
place in most conventional corporate structures. Still, the
obstacles to success are not inherent in the situation in
Japan, but are largely in the minds and behaviors of U.S.
and European companies.*
JAMES ABEGGLEN AND GEORGE STALK, JR.[1]

Gaishi (foreign-capital) company management is a popular subject
in Western books about Japan. However, as mentioned in Chapter
Nine, the focus of this topic has been skewed by an information
gap: although there are many American writers, very few writers
are Japanese. Speaking as a Japanese who worked for a *gaishi* company, I would like to explore some fundamental management issues of *gaishi* companies from a more cross-cultural perspective.

Major Concerns of *Gaishi* Managers

The following are the major concerns of *gaishi* managers according to the twenty-seventh survey of *gaishi* made by the Ministry of
International Trading and Industry (MITI).[2] Survey participants
were asked: "What makes the operation of *gaishi* difficult?" Their
answers were:

- Competition with Japanese companies (15 percent)
- Adjustment to the Japanese market (12 percent)

- Human resources strategy: hiring and keeping good resources (10 percent)
- High corporate taxes (9 percent)
- Japanese business traditions (9 percent)
- Communication with headquarters (6 percent)
- Do not see any difficulties (12 percent)
- Other (27 percent)

While the main question in the MITI survey focused on the difficulties of *gaishi* operations, in a different survey of 419 *gaishi* companies conducted by a management consulting firm, the main question was "What are the key factors for success?" Masaaki Atarashi, currently the vice president of Philips Japan, and formerly with Sara Lee Corporation, Shell Petroleum Company, the Coca-Cola Company, and Johnson & Johnson, analyzed the results of the survey to determine the key success factors in Japan for *gaishi* companies, as shown in Table 10.1.

Atarashi pointed out that the score correlated with customer satisfaction, "Matching products/services with market needs," which is one of the most important elements for any business, is very low at 16.2 percent. Many of the factors cited are connected to the relationship with headquarters, indicating that *gaishi* companies are focused more on their relationship with headquarters than on the relationship with their customers.[3] Atarashi notes that most of their attention is focused on internal concerns rather than on external strategic issues.[4]

We can confirm the validity of Atarashi's analysis by examining the MITI survey. The top three issues—competition, market adjustment, and hiring—eventually require support from headquarters. According to one human resources director of a *gaishi*, "Recruiting top-notch Japanese college graduates is not impossible. But the question is, how can we convince headquarters to spend at least the same amount of time and money as Japanese companies. They wouldn't understand." This is a frequent complaint, not only in regard to human resources, but also in the areas of marketing, product development, and quality assurance. When it comes to budgetary expenses, the discussion between American headquarters and the Japanese operations often becomes just a defense of positions rather than an attempt to develop a strategic

Table 10.1. Key Success Factors in Japan for *Gaishi* Companies.

Factor	Number of Companies	Percentage
1. Matching products and services with market needs	68	16.2
2. Operation by local staff members	56	13.3
3. Communication with headquarters	49	11.7
4. Understanding of and adjustment to Japanese business practices	48	11.5
5. Delegation from headquarters, autonomy of local management	48	11.5
6. Management by long-term strategy	41	9.8
7. Innovative, new products	30	7.2
8. Hiring and promoting good local personnel and managers	28	6.7
9. Managing the Japanese way	27	6.4
10. Support from headquarters	24	5.7
Total	419	100

Source: Adapted from Masaaki Atarashi, *Kokusai Business ni tsuyoku naru hou* (Developing an International Business Sense: Honing Your International Business Skills) (Tokyo: PHP Institute, 1993), pp. 120–121.

dialogue. It easily turns into a small U.S.–Japan trade negotiation, similar to those between government officers from the two countries. Quite often the two contingents begin talking about money before they have shared enough information. They do not even realize that they are not really communicating.

As we can see, even for common management issues shared by both Japanese companies in Japan and *gaishi,* the way of handling these issues is substantially different. A *gaishi* situation is more difficult and complex due to the fragile nature of the relationship between headquarters and the Japanese operation (Figure 10.1). In addition, Japanese management has a sense of unity with its employees, distributors, and customers. The importance of communication between American headquarters and Japanese operations,

Figure 10.1. Structural Impediments to *Gaishi* Communication.

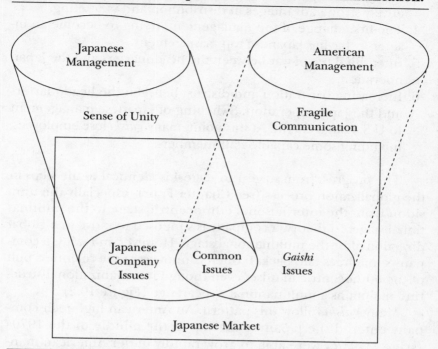

as well as between American expatriates and local Japanese staff members, cannot be overemphasized. Different perceptions of the Japanese market by American headquarters and Japanese operations and poor communications are the root causes of problems in managing *gaishi* operations in Japan.

Reinventing the *Gaishi* Roller Coaster

Kevin Jones, a partner at McKinsey Japan, provided a precise illustration of the six developmental stages, or the life cycle, of a *gaishi*:[5]

1. Entry by the leveraged new technology and/or product concept.
2. Rapid growth, but losing comparative advantages due to the competition with Japanese companies.

3. Reduction of profit ratio, because of Japanese companies' relatively strong advantages in distribution and marketing.
4. The first change of top management, trying to become an insider by having Japanese top management.
5. Intensified tug-of-war between the headquarters and the Japan operation.
6. Increasing frustration and distrust between the headquarters and the Japan operation. Switching of Japanese management to U.S. management. At this point, many *gaishi* lose employees, including some capable staff members.

The progress from stage 1 to stage 4 is identical to the steps in the globalization process (see Chapter Four), especially the transition from the international ethnocentric stage to the multinational stage. In theory, a company is supposed to move in a global direction after the multinational stage. However, in reality, a company sometimes falls back. It often cannot resist the relentless pull of the ethnocentric mindset even though its organizational structure maintains a multinational appearance (Figure 10.2).

Many *gaishi* follow this pattern. An American high-tech company entered the Japanese market in the middle of the 1970s (stage 1). They were able to grow rapidly under American management because of their product competitiveness, whereas Japanese companies were not able to produce the same performance (stage 2). In the early 1980s, the Japanese companies started introducing similar products into the market, which slowed the *gaishi's* growth (stage 3). As a countermeasure, the *gaishi* hired a Japanese managing director who was an expert in the field (the beginning of stage 4). Toward the end of the 1980s, the *gaishi* showed its second growth by reinforcing its vertical integration, including suppliers and wholesalers (stage 4). However, in 1991, its profit ratio started to drop because of the recession and intense price competition. The Japanese management tried to keep the current number of employees, while American headquarters ordered downsizing (stage 5). At the next stage, American headquarters switched the Japanese management back to American management (stage 6).

A crucial fact in such a pattern is that the market environment becomes much more difficult in the later stages than it was when the first American management was in charge of the *gaishi* operation.

Figure 10.2. Globalization: Theory Versus Reality.

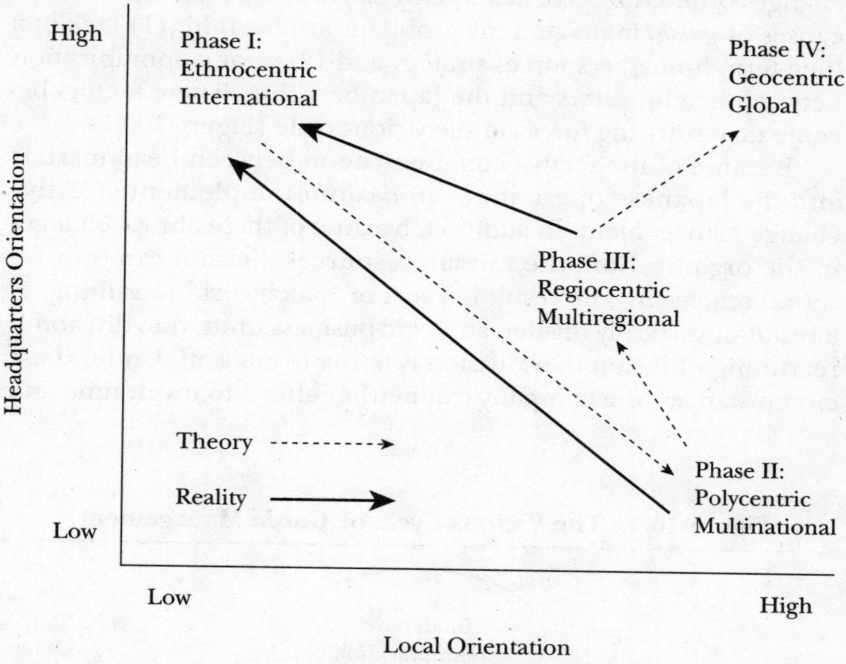

In addition, it must be realized that the more complex the organization becomes, the more important is the quality of communication between headquarters and the local operation. Some companies that do not realize these concerns simply reinvent the *gaishi* roller coaster, repeating the ups and downs caused by the changes in top management without solving the real problems. The fundamental question is how headquarters can enhance its relationship with the overseas operation. Beneath the obvious roller coaster lies a vicious cycle that negatively influences *gaishi* management.

The Vicious Cycle of *Gaishi* Management

As one of the very few voices representing over three hundred thousand Japanese who are working for *gaishi*, Reishi Ohtaki, director of William Mercer Limited of Japan, wrote about the organizational issues of *gaishi* management.[6] Addressing problems common to all *gaishi,* he first listed the confusion caused by frequent changes ordered by U.S. headquarters. He concluded that the root causes of *gaishi* management problems are twofold: (1) lack of a long-term human resources strategy and (2) poor communication between headquarters and the Japan branches. These factors become major driving forces in the vicious cycle (Figure 10.3).

Because of ineffective communication between headquarters and the Japanese operation, *gaishi* cannot implement effective change management. In addition, because of these abrupt changes in the organization, the human resources division can only respond reactively. The result is a sort of "patchwork" recruiting: as a result of vertically divided strategic business units, one division is recruiting while another division is trying to cut staff. Under these circumstances, the company can neither afford to invest time and

Figure 10.3. The Vicious Cycle of *Gaishi* Management.

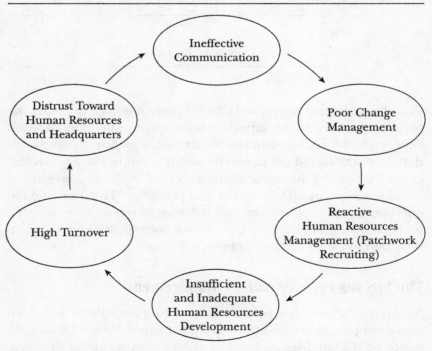

money in training nor integrate a human resources development system the way Japanese companies can. As a result, the company is unable to foster a sense of loyalty and often suffers from high turnover. Other divisions then start blaming the human resources division and U.S. headquarters—especially the marketing division, which is under pressure to meet sales targets.

The key to the success of a *gaishi* operation is management of the three interrelated "Cs" of change, communications, and context. Aligning change management is especially important because *gaishi* companies have to continually respond to global business and cultural transformations.

Aligning Change Management

Gaishi companies undergo more frequent changes than Japanese companies. These changes occur in the areas of strategic direction, new products, marketing plans, human resources policies, and organizational structures. The most critical areas of change concern Japanese top management and merger and acquisition or joint venture–related organizational changes.

Since the collapse of the bubble economy in Japan, many *gaishi* organizations have been facing drastic changes. Some have had to cancel major plans that were made during the bubble economy, such as initial public offerings in the Japanese market, office expansion, and capital investment in Japanese operations. *Gaishi* and Japanese companies are facing difficult turning points (see Chapter Eleven). However, *gaishi* are handicapped in their change management because of cultural variables regarding their perception of and attitudes toward change.

As we saw in Chapter Seven, according to Hofstede's cross-cultural management research, Japan is in the top seven of fifty countries on the uncertainty-avoidance index, while the United States is toward the bottom.[7] In other words, the degree of feeling threatened by an unknown situation, such as a drastic organizational change, is high in Japan and low in the United States. In general the Japanese, like many Asians, value continuity rather than change, while Americans value change rather than continuity. U.S. management tends to see change itself as a positive force. No wonder buzzwords such as "reengineering," "reinventing," and "reforming" are well accepted by American managers. In Japan, although reengineering has become a fad (more than twenty books about *rienjiniaringu* were published in 1993), the general attitude is one of skepticism about how to adjust to and soften drastic changes in Japanese organizations. I have met some Japanese managers who were seriously thinking about how to reinvent the organization without changing it. This does not mean that Japanese companies never change. It is a question of how the change is introduced. In order to manage change successfully, we have to be aware of its implications for communication as well as for context.

Change and Communication

Many management books and articles emphasize the importance of communication and the role of conversation in change management. For instance, Jeanie Duck, a vice president of the Boston Consulting Group, described the problem of lack of communication as follows:[8]

> When the task force chooses not to inform the rest of the organization about its work, it is saying, "We're busy figuring out your future—we'll tell you what it is when we're ready." Of course, people abhor information vacuums; when there is no on-going conversation as part of the change process, gossip fills the vacuum. Usually the rumors are much worse and more negative than anything that is actually going on.

In a cross-cultural organization, this problem easily occurs. Not many managers understand the important role of cross-cultural communication in change management. In *gaishi*, cross-cultural communication not only takes place between American expatriates and local Japanese staff members; it also involves the headquarters staff who deal with the Japanese operation through E-mail, fax, and tele- and videoconferencing. Thus, it is crucial to understand the impact of cross-cultural communication on change management.

First of all, we have to examine the communication in the pre-change phase. The key question is whether the existing communication is sufficient and efficient enough to absorb the unexpected change. In most cases, *gaishi* managers do not realize the value of daily communication until they encounter critical changes. If *gaishi* companies can create mutual trust between the U.S. and Japanese contingents, they can overcome the impact of any drastic change. Remember, conversation and communication can build trust.

A newly assigned director of an American chemical company provides a good model. The Japanese managers and the new director's American predecessor had had a communication problem. While all the Japanese managers spoke some English, it was not good enough for them to catch the nuanced details of the predecessor's English. The new director, aware of this problem, tried to improve the situation. He asked his secretary to attend as an interpreter for his first meeting with the Japanese managers. He opened the meeting with the remark: "Here, in this room, I'm the only one who speaks one language. Since I'd like to make sure that we understand each other well, please allow me to have an interpreter in this meeting." This statement impressed the Japanese managers because the American director had demonstrated that he cared about the quality of communications and had done it in such a nonoffensive way. His predecessor, on the other hand, had been a rapid speaker and had not used an interpreter. Because of their pride, the Japanese managers could not tell him that they needed an interpreter. For the first three months, the new American director conducted the meeting with an interpreter. By that time, the Japanese managers had begun to feel comfortable speaking in English because they had built mutual trust.

Second, communication during change management tends to be compressed and becomes a delicate issue. Inevitably, during change management, we have to face an important dilemma between communication and change management itself: information regarding organizational change is usually secret and, for this reason, communication tends to be restricted. As a result, communication that introduces changes from the U.S. contingent can become scant and abrupt. In turn, the Japanese become resentful and uncooperative. Under these conditions, neither side can set the stage for positive follow-up to the changes. This process accelerates the vicious cycle and augments the sense of distrust and negative energy in the organization.

The American director mentioned above also had a mission in regard to change management. On the first day of his fourth month in Japan, he had to announce an organizational change, which included closing one business unit. Although he worried about the reaction from the Japanese managers, he was able to make a smooth transition because of the trust that he had built. Some of the influential managers explained the meaning and the consequences of this organizational change to the other Japanese employees. At the same time, the American director showed enough effort to convince the Japanese employees of the necessity of the change by visiting all the branch offices with his interpreter.

The role of cross-cultural communication at an organizational level as well as at the individual level cannot be underestimated. Not only change agents, expatriates, local managers, and staff members but also everyone else involved has to acquire cross-cultural communication skills. In many cases, the Japanese side makes cultural issues an excuse for not accepting the changes. Applying the five core competencies to change management and managing context and communications appropriately enables the *gaishi* operation to keep cultural issues from becoming an excuse. It opens a constructive strategic dialogue with headquarters and encourages the implementation of proactive change management.

Context and Change

The subject of managing context vis-à-vis organizational culture is beginning to take center stage in management literature. However, this trend also reminds me of the cross-cultural impediments that affect U.S. management experts. As we saw in Chapter Two, U.S. management experts often forget their own cultural filters. Many write about organizational culture from an outsider's viewpoint in the belief that top management can change organizational culture. Again, organizations can look very different when viewed from the top rather than from the bottom, or by outsiders rather than by insiders. Also remember that although we cannot change a culture, we can facilitate the development of its identity.[9] It is not too much to say that inappropriate handling of change management in *gaishi* reflects the cross-cultural impediments facing U.S. management experts.

Once we develop contextual literacy about Japanese business practices, it becomes clear that Japanese management is not as bottom-up as is said. Instead, it is a middle-up and middle-down system, which seems like common sense to Japanese business-people. In fact, the Mitsubishi Research Institute is advocating what it calls a "soft system approach," which emphasizes strategic dia-logue among middle managers.[10] In the vertical Japanese corpo-rate structure, the *kacho* (section manager), *kacho dairi* (assistant section manager), and *shunin* (section chief) are key players whose jobs are to sense, guess, and respond to the requirements of upper management, as well as to oversee, motivate, and direct their sub-ordinates by means of a high-context communication style.

The power of middle managers in *gaishi* is also very important. The Japanese employees in *gaishi* bring their mindsets into their organizations from their previous experience in Japanese corpo-rations. A major problem in change management in *gaishi* is the strong resistance of middle managers in the Japanese operation if they are not appropriately involved in the process. Such resistance is often subtle. The Japan branch is able to manipulate the ap-pearance of change—*tatemae* change—without really doing any-thing substantial. After a while, those in U.S. headquarters realize that nothing has actually changed in the Japanese operation and begin to feel that they are being fooled. They cannot understand that what is actually going on in the change management process.

The role of the middle managers cannot be underestimated in change management, a fact that was well understood by the newly assigned director of the *gaishi* chemical company mentioned above. When he announced the company's organizational change, he also formed a task force of middle managers to decide on their resource allocation. Such activities provided the Japanese man-agers with a sense of inclusion.

The Role of Change Agents

In addition to the involvement of middle managers, the entire process of change management has to be reexamined based on the five core competencies. The role of the change agent is extremely important here, whether it is in the form of a newly assigned top-management team in the Japanese operation, a task-force com-mittee such as a transitional management team or a steering committee, or a consultant. The key is whether the change agent has cross-cultural business literacy and therefore can read the context of the Japanese organization precisely and convert it into coherent content for the U.S. management, which naturally asks for high-content explanations. All of the change agents need to apply culturally sensitive management processes to the entire project. They have to know how to modify the process in light of the differing perceptions of change management. In addition, they must be aware of the nature of the cross-cultural organization; they need an excellent sense of organizational dynamics; and they have to know how to facilitate a cross-cultural work team (see Chapter Five).

It can be disastrous to *gaishi* organizations to have a change agent who is no more than *eigoya*. *Eigoya* is Japanese slang; its direct translation is "a store of English." It refers to a Japanese who is a good speaker of English and gets along with American expatriates or visitors, but who does not have any business skills in a non–English-speaking environment. An MBA alone is not a sufficient qualification for a change agent in a cross-cultural organization like a *gaishi*. In general, such people are good at content analysis (data, quantitative information, and so on). It is easy for them to satisfy U.S. expatriates. However, some of them, especially those who do not have working experience in Japanese organizations, are not always competent when dealing with contextual issues (interpersonal issues, relationships, or soft issues). At the same time, they are vulnerable to the bias of the Japanese employees. They are likely to be labeled *eigoya* unless they can prove their contextual ability. The change agent has to practice HCHC management by applying culturally sensitive management processes, communicating with both Japanese and Americans, and shifting his or her own style and perception.

Developing Contextual Literacy

The challenge for *gaishi* involves fundamental questions regarding the management styles of the two countries. As we saw in Chapter Seven, Japanese management style can be characterized as high-context and U.S. management style as high-content. As many scholars and consultants have said,[11] in general, Japanese companies tend to stress context while U.S. companies tend to focus on content. I realize now that my first year working at Toshiba after I finished school trained me to become contextually literate in business.

Before visiting corporate clients, my boss (a *kacho dairi,* an assistant section manager) told me to gather information about the people we were going to meet, including their hobbies, year of graduation, school, family structure, and past relations with Toshiba (information that is easily accessible in Japan). This information provides contextual material that seems peripheral from an American manager's perspective, but that is very significant. As part of my ongoing, on-the-job training, after visiting clients with my boss I had to write the minutes of the meeting and interpret all the subtle nuances and clues that the client showed. My boss would not accept the minutes until I was able to read the context correctly and figure out what was going on behind the clients' actual statements. For instance, one client asked us, "How is Yamamoto-san (the division manager) doing these days?" I thought it was just a greeting. Then I learned that the client was implying that we should have visited with Yamamoto-san because the client thought that our positions were not high enough to discuss the project.

In my first year at Toshiba, I was like a *gaijin.* Joining a Japanese company and working closely with someone like my boss, I developed my literacy in Japanese business practices. This training is surprising to American businesspeople. Many social psychologists have pointed out that we must go back to our childhood to find the roots of cultural learning. Similarly, without undergoing rigorous corporate training—whether formal or informal—we cannot become competent in Japanese business communities.

As we can see from the differences in communication styles, it is difficult for U.S. managers to get contextual information (for example, their Japanese colleague's nonverbal communication or the undocumented history of a relationship with a Ministry of Finance officer) and manage it appropriately. On the other hand, many Japanese managers are convinced that they do not have to contentualize their contextual information, because they take it for granted. Thus, in *gaishi,* managing the context is the major challenge for U.S. managers, while managing content (especially the quarterly sales budget and return on investment) is the challenge for Japanese managers, as we shall see in the next chapter.

Chapter Eleven

Japanese Companies in the United States

Another, even greater, challenge facing Japan is how to cope with the coming de-massification of a society that has been propagandized into believing that homogeneity is always a virtue. . . . As Japan enters the Third Wave era it will face potentially explosive heterogeneous pressures.
ALVIN TOFFLER[1]

In today's global market, we see Japanese products almost everywhere. Given this fact, can we conclude that Japanese companies are really global? In this chapter, we begin to unveil the cross-cultural challenges for Japanese corporations beneath their strong product image.

The Performance of Japanese Companies Outside Japan

Contrary to popular opinion regarding U.S.–Japan trade, Japanese manufacturers abroad have a smaller profit ratio than American companies in Japan. A fiscal 1991 survey by the Ministry of International Trading and Industry indicated that Japanese manufacturers abroad have a 0.9 percent profit ratio while *gaishi* manufacturers in Japan have a 4.6 percent ratio.[2] In fact, the profit ratio of Japanese companies in the United States (−1.9 percent) is lower than in Europe (−0.6 percent) and in Asia (4.8 percent). One reason for this lower ratio is that Japanese corporate strategy tends to emphasize expanding market share, which suppresses the profit ratio. But that is not the main reason. The survey also shows that the companies that entered overseas markets no later than 1985 have started to make a profit, whereas those that did so after 1986 are still in the red. This finding suggests that many Japanese corporations have not had enough experience managing overseas operations.

Because these corporations are still struggling with managing their own overseas operations, it is much harder for them to acquire other companies abroad. Kenichi Ohmae, former director of McKinsey Japan, noted that, according to their research, only 5 percent of Japanese companies' cross-border acquisitions were rated a success.[3] This figure is one-sixth the rate of European and American companies. In contrast to the internationally invincible image that Japanese products enjoy, the Japanese companies that produce them still have a long way to go to become truly global corporations.

Let's start with the same question, "What are the key factors for success in the U.S. market for Japanese companies?" that we asked for *gaishi* in Chapter Ten. A survey jointly conducted by the University of Michigan, Egon-Zender International, and the Sanno Institute of Business Administration during a seven-month period from September 1988 to March 1989 sheds light on the issues of American managers working for *nikkei kigyo,* Japanese companies in the United States.[4] Regarding the question, "What are the key factors for success for *nikkei kigyo?*" American managers working for Japanese companies responded as follows:

Factor	Percentage
Quality of products and services	32
Quality of managers and employees	14
Distribution and price	12
Management ability	10
Support from headquarters	7
Image and reputation	6
Long-term strategy	5
Other	14

Compared to the key success factors of *gaishi,* these results seem more straightforward. Authentic strategic issues, such as product, price, promotion, and place, account for nearly 50 percent of the factors. However, human resources–related items (quality of managers and employees and management ability) account for 24 percent. In the survey's research interview, many American managers commented that Japanese companies are far behind in their development of human resources systems in the multinational context.[5] Although many U.S. scholars admire the Japanese human resources system, their views are valid only when looking at the Japanese domestic environment and not for Japanese corporations abroad.

Interestingly enough, a survey on *nikkei kigyo* in Europe finds the highest correlation between the management ability of Japanese managers and the job satisfaction of their European employees. If the Japanese management ability is high, the job satisfaction rate is also high.[6] In Europe and the United States, many employees are frustrated with Japanese managers' lack of clear goal setting, feedback, performance appraisal, and other management behaviors.[7] During my empirical research at the American Graduate School of International Management concerning Japanese companies in the United States, I repeatedly heard the same complaints from American employees about Japanese managers:

"They don't explain why."

"I don't know what they want me to do."

"They don't know how to say 'Thank you' to their subordinates."

"They call too many meetings, but reach no conclusions."

"They suddenly become very emotional and start reprimanding us."

On the other hand, Japanese managers had these complaints about the American employees:

"They are not sensitive to other people's needs and requirements (*Ki ga kikanai*). I have to spell out everything."

"How can they expect promotion so quickly without trying to study Japanese?"

"They only seem able to learn by analyzing all the time."

As we have seen, these comments exemplify the typical cross-cultural communication problems caused by not knowing the cultural variables and how to manage them. Many surveys show that Japanese managers do not realize that they are not communicating effectively with host country workers. Some Japanese managers, as well as some American managers, do not pay any attention to the quality of communication.

However, there are two critical differences between *gaishi* and *nikkei kigyo* that are more significant than the differences in power structure (that is, in *gaishi*, Americans are the owners and have the power, while in *nikkei kigyo*, the Japanese have the power). These two issues are:

1. *Asymmetrical development in the process of globalization:* Japanese companies have not succeeded in developing themselves as global organizations in the same way that they have with production. While the Japanese management style in the area of production, including the use of quality circles and just-in-time systems, is highly regarded by American management, the management systems for white-collar workers, such as the seniority system and lifetime employment, are perceived as specific to Japan and are not well regarded.

2. *Leadership gap:* Japanese managers lack leadership experience in multicultural environments. Usually, when a Japanese manager is transferred to an overseas branch, his or her new position will be higher than it was in Japan. For instance, a section manager may become a general manager at the subsidiary. However, Japanese expatriates seldom receive high-content management training, such as enrollment in an MBA program, relying instead on a high-context management style, such as relationship building. As we saw, context is culture-specific. Consequently, it is difficult for Japanese managers to demonstrate their leadership to non-Japanese subordinates.

Tackling these two issues should be the top priority for Japanese companies. But many Japanese managers only pay attention to obvious problems, such as the increasing number of lawsuits brought by American workers suing for discrimination or sexual harassment, rather than dealing with the larger issues. Japanese managers do need to develop an awareness and understanding of the American legal environment. However, unless they focus on the underlying issues of asymmetrical development in globalization and the leadership gap, we will continue to see the same problems arising.

Japanese Globalization: An Asymmetrical Development Process

In *gaishi,* the major communication issues occur between U.S. headquarters and the Japan operation, although there are miscommunication problems at an individual level between American expatriates and Japanese employees. On the other hand, in *nikkei kigyo,* it is not *inter*organizational communications (those between Japan headquarters and the U.S. subsidiary) that cause problems as much as *intra*organizational communications (those within the U.S. subsidiary). This does not mean that Japanese companies have better headquarters-subsidiary communications. The reality is that Japanese companies have not yet reached the stage where their subsidiaries are becoming more autonomous and therefore are undertaking a tug-of-war with their headquarters in Tokyo (as many *gaishi* operations do with their American headquarters).

Historically, American companies are much more experienced in overseas markets than Japanese companies. Many American companies are at the multinational and multiregional stages of globalization, described in Chapter Four. Japanese organizations, in contrast to the high availability of their products worldwide, are behind in achieving globalization. In other words, their development has been asymmetrical. It's no wonder that Japanese companies have started to have problems with American white-collar workers while, at the same time, their management style has been appreciated by American blue-collar workers.

By examining the history of Japanese corporations in the global marketplace,[8] we can understand why the Japanese lag in developing global organizations. Major Japanese companies began to export their products in the 1950s and 1960s. In the 1970s, they started direct investment and manufacturing. However, it was not until the mid-1980s that they moved toward multinational operations. In the last ten years they have rushed to become quasiglobal companies, but they still lack experience. In addition, the driving force behind the globalization of Japanese companies was reactive: to avoid "trade friction" or to respond to *Yen-daka* (strong yen). In contrast, American and European companies have had more proactive reasons for globalizing, such as transferring advanced technology.

The Leadership Gap

The second critical difference between *gaishi* and *nikkei kigyo* is the leadership gap between Japanese managers and the expectations of their American employees. As indicated in the above survey, the management ability of Japanese managers is questioned by American as well as European employees. This leadership gap involves three cultural variables: communication style, management style, and language:

1. *Communication style:* Most of the criticism of Japanese managers abroad can be attributed to their high-context communication style. As we have seen, to American workers, Japanese managers seem to be vague, unclear, and illogical.

2. *Management style:* In Japanese companies, because of their group-oriented mindset, managers are not trained to stand alone and lead directly, which is what American workers expect from their managers. In addition, Japanese managers are most effective when they are in a high-context environment—that is, working in the same organization over a long period of time, developing a network where they know each person's strengths, and rotating their jobs periodically, which fosters a broad contextual knowledge of the organization. However, when they are in a context-free environment (that is, a high-content environment), they are not as effective.

3. *Language:* As we saw in Chapter Three, many Japanese managers abroad are not competent at communicating in English. Japanese companies generally use the Test of English for International Communication (TOEIC). Jointly developed by the Educational Testing Service and the Japanese government, this test requires 700 as the minimum score for overseas assignment, which is difficult to achieve for someone who has not lived abroad. In addition to incompetence in English, there is

also a tendency toward "*eigo* [English]-phobia," or a fear of English. These seeming inadequacies restrain Japanese managers from approaching the challenges of cross-cultural communication in a more holistic way. Many Japanese managers are so preoccupied with their English and their TOEIC score that it is difficult for them to consider the other fundamental issues mentioned above. They tend to say, "If only I could speak English, I would not have any problems." They do not see the crucial role that cultural issues play.

Thus, a vicious cycle forms in *nikkei kigyo* management, as shown in Figure 11.1. Because of ineffective communication between Japanese managers and American workers, the Japanese managers' different management styles make American workers feel uncomfortable, thus creating a leadership gap on the part of the Japanese managers. In particular, the Japanese managers are not good at providing feedback and delegation to American workers, which frustrates the American workers. As a result, *nikkei kigyo* experience high turnover because their American workers are unmotivated. A sense of distrust then develops between the Japanese managers and the American workers. At this stage, they do not make an effort to communicate with each other.

A Turning Point for Japanese Management

Just as American companies and managers need to focus on the five core competencies and the seven mental disciplines in order to enhance their global organizations, so must Japanese companies and managers. The need is urgent for Japanese corporations because of the inevitability of the changes occurring in the global business environment. Under the post-bubble-economy recession, Japanese companies have had to face one of the most important turning points since World War II. This shift has been caused by the following three key multidimensional issues.

1. *Structural changes in industry:* Japanese companies are moving from providing mass-produced, standardized products to more highly value-added products and services. One epoch-making event took place when Nintendo (with approximately 850 employees)

Figure 11.1. The Vicious Cycle of *Nikkei Kigyo* Management.

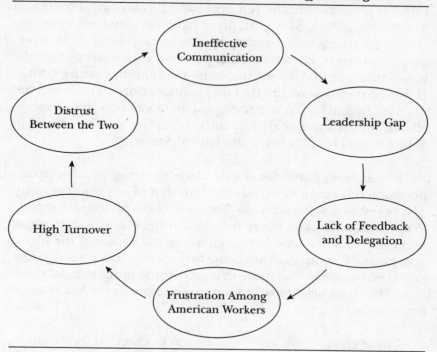

surpassed Matsushita Electric/Panasonic (with approximately 48,000 employees) in fiscal 1993 current profit. Panasonic is one of the companies that has symbolized the mass-production capability of Japan Inc. A key paradigm is the "water philosophy," which means making products as available as water—that is, accessible and cheap. Under this paradigm, the discussion-intensive, group-oriented characteristics of the Japanese management system complement the requirements of a centralized, export-based strategy. However, the trend of structural change toward more value-added, locally differentiated products and services is requiring companies to become more multinational in their organization.[9] In other words, Japanese corporations are being forced to give up their Japan-centered systems and to strive toward becoming global organizations.

2.   *A chronic trade imbalance and a strong yen:* In 1993, when the rapid appreciation of the yen broke the psychological barrier of $1 = ¥100 (in 1995, $1 = ¥79), many Japanese managers were concerned for their survival and stopped worrying about shifting production overseas. For a long time, Japanese management held the belief that, ideally, Japan should be the manufacturing center. However, they now realize that they cannot afford to maintain this doctrine because of an increasing gap in labor costs (for example, Nissan Motor Co. decided to shift the entire production of its Sentra model from Japan to the United States).[10]

3.   *An aging population and the upcoming shortage of labor:* Japan's population is aging more rapidly than that of any other country. The population will peak in 2007 and will begin to decrease slowly.[11] Preparations must be made for the coming chronic shortage of domestic labor. As a result, in addition to the impact of the strong yen, Japanese companies are being forced to abandon their Japan-centered paradigm and move in a polycentric multinational direction. They have also started to put more emphasis on Asia than on other areas.

These changes are not being driven by external forces alone. Japanese corporations are also being challenged because of their high-context management style.

Rethinking High-Context Management

Akio Morita, the cofounder of Sony Corporation, in a controversial article written in 1992,[12] initiated a rethinking of the old Japanese management paradigm. In contrast to the old philosophy, "Better products for less," which is exemplified in the water philosophy, Morita advocated its antithesis, "Better products for the deserved price." Given this new paradigm, Japanese companies could increase the financial return to their shareholders as well as to their employees. At the same time, many Japanese started rethinking the extreme focus on relationships in doing business because of several scandals involving politicians and private industries, including securities houses and construction companies. Furthermore, the low productivity of Japanese white-collar workers started to be questioned. An analysis showed that, in fact, the high productivity of blue-collar workers subsidized the cost of white-collar employees.[13] *Nemawashi* ("to lay the groundwork") costs could no longer be ignored. For instance, Hitachi Ltd. calculated that it spent ¥1,700 million (approximately $170 million) on its budget process alone.[14] It also required the involvement of twenty-eight thousand managers. Such are the drawbacks of an overly consensus-oriented decision-making process.

In addition, the high-context communication style of middle and senior managers is also in jeopardy. Although the issue of the generation gap repeats throughout human history, it is true that today many younger Japanese employees are having difficulty communicating with the older generation.[15] The traditional Japanese tacit understanding is not working with younger employees. Many young Japanese have commented that their bosses should spell out everything.

The difference between today and fifteen years ago is a power shift in which old authority is losing power as a result of the information revolution, as predicted by Alvin Toffler.[16] There are two reasons for this shift. The first is the easy accessibility of information. Information flows two ways. Today there are more opportunities not only to receive information but also to express opinions. As a result, young Japanese can criticize the older-generation bosses in media such as weekly magazines. They have harsh words for their high-context, "wishy-washy" managers. Fifteen years ago, I heard the same kinds of complaints at Toshiba. But at that time there were few opportunities to express such thoughts and feelings openly. By voicing their difficulties in working with the older generation, the younger generation can keep its freer style and will not have to adapt to tradition as did previous generations.

Second, Japanese business communities are also facing power shifts caused by diversity issues. Although slow by American standards, this trend is happening rapidly enough to make the older generation of Japanese uncomfortable. One aspect of the new diversity concerns the role of women. Again, this change is very slow, but we are beginning to see increasing numbers of working women who do more than just serve tea in the workplace. Another diversity issue concerns non-Japanese workers. They still represent a very small percentage of the forty-five million Japanese workers. However, the increase has caused insecurities for older Japanese, who are used to working in homogeneous environments. *A low-context communication style rather than a high-context one works best in heterogeneous groups.* Thus, many Japanese managers now have to learn how to communicate clearly even while they are in Japan. Rather than complaining, *"Kiga kikanai"* ("Those guys are insensitive"), they have to expand and elaborate the content so that other low-context employees can understand.

From *Kokusaika* to Transcultural Management: Changing Mindsets

One of the most overused clichés in Japan is *kokusaika* ("internationalization"). Because of Japan's relatively short history of international diplomacy and its historically rare interactions with foreigners, *kokusaika* has become a nationwide slogan, both in the private sector and in government organizations. Some Japanese think that *kokusaika* means only to be able to speak English. Others think that it also means to buy foreign goods.

Recently, *uchi naru kokusaika* ("internal internationalization") has become popular. It involves inviting foreigners into the organization in order to foster diversity. In the late 1980s, many Japanese companies started employing foreign workers to make up for the shortage of labor during the bubble economy. However, as is often the case, there was a kind of tokenism in many organizations, which promoted a few *gaijin* managers and then claimed that they were international companies. In 1992 Nemic Lambda, a switching manufacturer, assigned a Malaysian national as CEO of its Japanese headquarters, thus capturing media attention.[17] Such attention indicates that in reality this case is still an exception to the rule.

As we have seen, Japanese companies are at the stage where they no longer can merely pay lip service to *kokusaika*. They now know that they cannot survive unless they promote internationalization and globalization. One important point dismissed by many Japanese *kokusaika* activists is the need to change mindsets—to shift into the geocentric mode and practice the full range of the five core transcultural competencies and the seven mental disciplines. With regard to its understanding and awareness of organizational culture and national cultures, Japan is even further behind than the United States. It is not only a matter of introducing some new systems and structures; Japan must also look deeper. As a result, some companies have started more active human resources practices and are providing intercultural training programs for overseas assignees.

For instance, one common human resources practice held in *nikkei kigyo* is "double casting." A Japanese manager and an American manager are assigned to the same position and are given slightly different titles. The Japanese intention in introducing double casting is to emphasize teamwork; however, this system is also sometimes perceived by American managers as Japanese interference. Another more informal but similar practice is the "buddy system," in which a Japanese and an American are paired for day-to-day interactions, such as attending meetings. A key objective of the two practices is to promote mutual support and team learning by having employees work in pairs. In reality, these systems sometimes do and sometimes do not work. When participants cannot communicate effectively and build mutual trust, they tend to become suspicious of the system itself. As a result, some people believe that double casting is a way of introducing shadow managers to keep non-Japanese managers in token positions; this leads to the "Japanese conspiracy" theory.[18] Japanese managers have to remember that what differentiates double casting from shadow managers is the quality of daily interaction and communications.

Recently in Japan, intercultural management issues have started to receive more attention, although not as much as in the United States. Some influential scholars have introduced the concept of intercultural management.[19] Some companies place globalization as their top strategic agenda. For instance, Mitsubishi Corporation began a global human resources development program that allows employees to work across national boundaries rather than to belong to specific national operations. This program is the first such trial among Japanese companies.[20] There is no doubt that the key to success in the twenty-first century for Japanese companies will be to manage cultural diversity in both their overseas and domestic operations.

Chapter Twelve

United States–Japan Alliance Management

When we reached the agreement after months of
negotiation, we thought it the end of the worst part.
Now, I say that was the beginning.
A MANAGER INVOLVED WITH A CROSS-BORDER ALLIANCE

Despite the fact that global strategic alliances have been a common strategic option in international business and that the number of alliances is increasing, we still see many failures. According to a June 1994 article in *International Business,* half of these cross-border alliances fail. During 1993, when the recession in Japan started sowing doubts about the Japanese economy, a number of joint ventures terminated, even though some had been in existence for over forty years.[1]

When Hershey Foods Corporation closed its joint venture relationship with Fujiya, a Japanese candy maker, one of the American senior executives said, "We had different philosophies and priorities."[2] Such statements are not unusual in the context of U.S.–Japan alliances. Nor is it a coincidence that I have often heard statements similar to the following:[3]

"We could not get along, which destroyed our co-operative spirit."
"We came from two disparate corporate cultures."
"Managers within the joint venture could not work with the owners' managers."

"The contributions of our partner did not meet our expectations."
"We could not get our staff down the line to deliver what we
had promised."

Such comments exemplify the difficulties in achieving cross-cultural collaboration and in making alliances work. In working to achieve success, one well-known U.S.–Japan alliance spent over fifty million dollars yearly in round-trip air tickets between the United States and Japan, an amount that signals a major commitment. The effort involved in making an alliance work can be arduous, as well as requiring large amounts of time and money. Most companies realize this. On the other hand, according to Kenichi Ohmae, "There is also an impression that alliances represent, at best, a convenience, a quick-dirty means of entry into foreign markets. These attitudes make managers skittish and impatient."[4] As a result, those involved don't realize some of their critical blind spots.

Blind Spots of the Cross-Border Strategic Alliance

Most blind spots—not only in U.S.–Japan joint ventures but also in other cross-border alliances—arise from three specific situations, the "triple culture gap." First is national culture. As we have seen, critical differences in national character make it difficult for organizations to work together across national borders. The tendency to be group-oriented or individualistic, vertical or horizontal, and risk-avoiding or risk-taking may aggravate contentions or inhibit creativity.

The second gap concerns industry culture. Each industry has its own perceptions and business style that comprise its culture. When different industries join together through mergers, joint ventures, or other alliances, these unique perceptions and styles may clash. Increasing numbers of cross-industry alliances are taking place: for instance, Read Rite, a Silicon Valley–based high-tech electronics company, entered into a joint venture with Sumitomo Metal, a traditional Japanese steel company, and Applied Materials, a semiconductor manufacturer, began an alliance with Komatsu, a Japanese machinery manufacturer. Each of these industries functions according to its own culture: a semiconductor manufacturer requires quick decision making because of a short product cycle and intense competition, while a steel manufacturer requires long-term investment planning because of its capital-intense nature.

The third gap is in the area of corporate culture, which reflects the norms, assumptions, and values about business practices that corporate members share. As we saw in Chapter Two, despite the recent attention given to the topic of corporate culture, American management literature has traditionally paid little attention to the connection between corporate and national cultures. The popular press has implied that excellent companies have strong corporate cultures; however, the link between a strong culture and strong performance can be challenged.[5] While strong corporate cultures can bring many benefits to corporations, there are drawbacks as well. What will happen when two companies that have strong corporate cultures form an alliance, particularly when the two companies are from significantly different cultural contexts? Even if we discount all the national cultural differences that influence our underlying assumptions, consider the different corporate cultural backgrounds of American and Japanese companies: different product cycles, decision-making processes, degrees of formality, size, and company history. These areas are all potential causes of clashes between corporate cultures.

The triple culture gap quite often prevents both American and Japanese management teams from completing a project according to the original and optimistic plan. Differences in communication style and language often aggravate expectations, perceptions, and assumptions regarding:

- Strategic intent (vision, goal, and time frame)
- Operational processes (implementation and decision making)
- Information sharing
- Resource allocation

Once again, differences and gaps could become great resources, if only they were managed well—which they can be, as we will see below.

How Shared Vision Can Cross Cultures

Management consultants and scholars emphasize the value of having shared vision—an indispensable element in any strategic alliance. Both parties must also have mutual respect. However, many managers—both American and Japanese—merely stay at the surface level of shared vision and mutual respect (*tatemae* vision and *tatemae* respect). Considering the nature of cross-cultural organizations, in cross-border alliances the process of gaining shared vision is even more important than the vision itself.

Figure 12.1 illustrates a key framework for a successful alliance and contains several critical messages. A U.S.–Japan alliance needs to bridge all the cultural differences, including the triple culture gap. To do so requires a new set of rules and a shared strategic intent, which together act as a solid and stable central support based on the common ground of the two countries. I have seen some cases in which the managers gave up their attempt to create this central support before they had acknowledged and established the common ground. In other cases they assumed that the central support had been firmly built only to realize that it was just floating in the water. In order to support the bridge, the two foundations, which are deeply rooted in each culture, are vital. In other words, an understanding of the cultural traits of others and an objective

Figure 12.1. Management of Cross-Cultural Alliances.

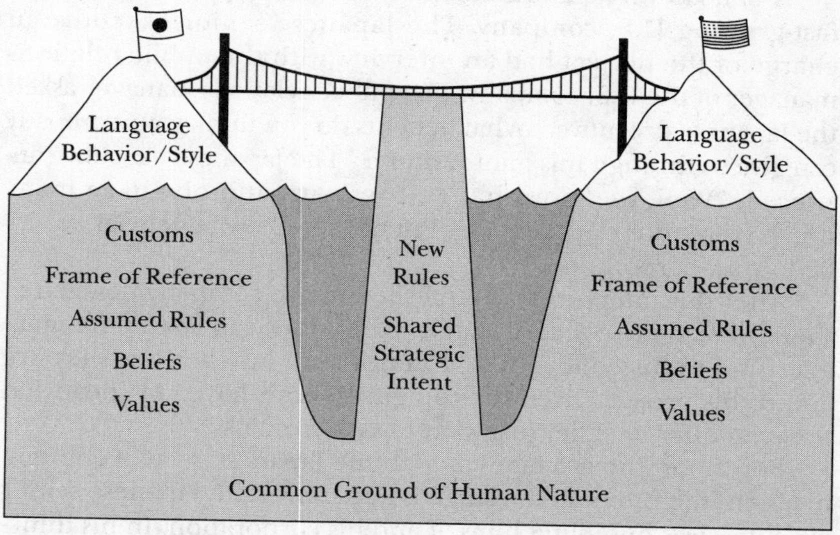

Language
Behavior/Style

Customs

Frame of Reference

Assumed Rules

Beliefs

Values

New
Rules

Shared
Strategic
Intent

Language
Behavior/Style

Customs

Frame of Reference

Assumed Rules

Beliefs

Values

Common Ground of Human Nature

Source: Geonexus Communications, Inc. Copyright © 1994 by Geonexus Communications, Inc. Reproduced by permission.

awareness of our own culture and value system are basic requirements for a successful alliance.

The difference between a successful alliance and a failed one is only minimal in the beginning. It is like the point of departure of two railroads. Although they are running in the same direction at first, they eventually bring the organization to totally different destinations. Masazumi Ishii, managing director of AZCA Inc. and an expert in management of cross-border alliances, puts it acutely:[6]

> The process of alliance decline begins from day one—in which differences in expectations between the partners lead to frequent staff changes, meaning less commitment, translating to less allocation of resources, in turn fostering less trust in the partner, thus leading to a cyclical process of breakdown and subsequently failure.

The Role of Communications in Alliances

As we saw in *gaishi* and *nikkei kigyo,* the role of communication is crucial, and it is also a critical element in alliances. Even a small miscommunication may sow the seeds of doubt and distrust between partners, as the following example indicates.

A well-known Japanese company started a joint venture with a fast-growing U.S. company. The Japanese senior executive in charge of the project had an interview with the public relations manager of the U.S. company. The public relations manager asked the Japanese executive, "What benefits do you think your company can give us through this joint venture?" The Japanese executive answered, "Well, we know that we can learn and obtain so many things from your company. But I'm not sure how beneficial we can be to your corporation."

After this interview was published in the company newsletter, there were some concerns among the American staff. One manager said to his colleagues, "I'm not sure how serious they are about this project. Even the top guy doesn't have any idea what they can offer us. They just want to take from us."

For those who are familiar with the Japanese style of communication, the intended message is apparent. The Japanese senior executive was humbling himself and his corporation. In his thinking, talking about the benefits of his corporation might be perceived as arrogant. But this miscommunication is not only a matter of the American manager's lack of understanding of the Japanese. The Japanese senior executive also should have been sensitive to how his words would be interpreted. Thus, in order to make cross-border alliances work, both parties have to be aware of pitfalls within the triple culture gap. The following tips should help prevent alliance breakdown and promote transcultural success.

Tips for Successful Alliances

I'd like to start with the big picture. Howard Perlmutter and David Heenan state that the health of global strategic partners depends on whether the participating companies can learn and share new skills.[7] They summarize six areas that deserve special attention:

1. *Mission:* Each partner must believe that the other has something it needs. Top executives and divisional managers must convince middle managers and affiliates on both sides to build on strengths and reduce weaknesses.
2. *Strategy:* Multinational corporations sometimes rush into a partnership, hoping that a synergistic plan will somehow evolve. But strategy must come first. Partners must avoid "niche collision," which occurs when separate deals produce an untenable overlap between cooperation and competition.
3. *Governance:* Contrary to Americans' tendency to believe that power, not parity, should govern collaborative ventures, Europeans and Japanese often consider partners as equals, subscribe to management by consensus, and rely on lengthy discussion to secure a stronger commitment to shared enterprises.
4. *Culture:* An important factor in the endurance of a global alliance is cultural chemistry. The partners must be willing to mold a common set of values, styles, and structure while retaining their national identities.
5. *Organization:* The new approach to partnerships mandates new organizational patterns. Both parties have to maintain new organizational methods to deal with the logistical complexities.
6. *Management:* An alliance partner changes the nature of daily decision making and places new pressures on an enterprise. Before formalizing any coalition, multinational corporations must identify these operational issues, which range from transfer pricing to personnel matters.

Alliance management can be demonstrated by an example. When an American electronics company started an alliance with a Japanese electronics company to develop a new product, it paid a great deal of attention to the above six areas. First, the company established a cross-functional task force for the alliance project. The task force included one controller who was in charge of the alliance, three senior engineers, one production manager, the human resources director, and one organization development (OD) specialist; they studied many cases of cross-cultural alliance and decided to focus on the following questions:

1. What is the goal of this alliance? What is the significance to both companies of achieving that goal?
2. What are the potential obstacles to achieving that goal?
3. How do the companies check progress toward the goal?
4. How do they decide on resource allocation?

In addition, the OD specialist advised the team to focus on invisible assets. (According to Vladimir Pucik, an associate professor at Cornell University, companies should focus more on invisible assets than on visible assets.[8]) The task force added the following three questions:

1. What are the critical differences in the companies' work styles, norms, and values? What are the similarities?
2. What kinds of guidelines are required for their communications?
3. How should they resolve conflicts when they arise?

Two months before the alliance was announced, the task force shared these key questions with a contingent from the Japanese company and started to discuss the issues. Prior to this, a contingent from the American company had learned Japanese business practices, communication styles, and key cultural variables, such as different attitudes toward conflict and the strong conflict avoidance of the Japanese. The Japanese contingent learned the flip side—how to do business with Americans. The American contingent focused particularly on language modification because there were only two English speakers among the six members of the Japanese contingent.

One outcome of this joint preparatory session was that eight members—four Japanese and four Americans—formed the transitional committee that would check on progress and mediate conflict. The transitional committee gathered information regarding teamwork, communications, and conflicts from employees, both American and Japanese. It invited each unit to a monthly feedback session to share the information and reestablish guidelines for communications, decision making, and meeting management. Such efforts at mediation helped the alliance to maintain a productive and healthy atmosphere. One American engineer involved with many cross-border alliances commented, "In the beginning, I thought we were just wasting time. But, now I can see differences from what I have done before. We should have taken these steps before."

As we saw in this case, mutual learning between the partners and feedback are important elements in solidifying the alliance. As a summary, the following practical advice is useful for any alliance.

Focus for the First Six Months

In the early stages of an alliance, both parties have to accomplish much in a limited time. Key tasks include the following:

- *Clarify values and align beliefs:* Both parties clarify their values and belief systems so that they can minimize gaps in expectations, perceptions, and assumptions.
- *Clarify strategic intent:* Both parties have to communicate and clarify their strategic intent and build the shared strategic intent of the new alliance. This includes setting goals, adjusting time frames, and clarifying and confirming operational processes such as decision making, the reporting system, and information sharing.

In addition to the strategic issues above, many human resources issues must be addressed in the early stages. One of the most fertile areas for future conflict in the alliance is how resources are allocated. However, quite often the human resources division is not involved in the initial planning stage before the formation of the alliance and it is then obliged to handle human resources issues in reactive ways. It is therefore especially important that the human resources division focus on the following issues:

- *Develop a joint human resources training strategy:* A Toshiba human resources expert involved in a triad alliance realized the impact of culture clashes when he said, "We should have made more cooperative efforts with human resources people from Siemens and IBM and developed joint programs."[9] What companies can do, as we saw in the above case of successful alliance management, is to include human resources managers in the early stage of planning. They should prepare both hard (technical) training programs and soft (cultural) programs.
- *Clarify human resources policies as much as possible:* Issues related to the transfer of competencies (for example, personnel exchange) especially need to be addressed in the initial agreements.[10]

Alliances have to deal with many critical issues and tasks in the first six months. The number of people involved with the project rapidly increases during this period. It takes time for them to adjust to the new working environment, especially if it is a cross-cultural workplace. Some of them may encounter culture shock even though they do not leave their home country. Many surveys show that in the first six months people tend to go through culture shock cycles.[11] Those who are in the new cultural environment may feel frustration and anger. During this period, they tend to blame the other culture. Even in management development programs, global managers may experience initial shock and midprogram frustration and anxiety about the team process.[12] Many Japanese businesspeople feel that they need at least half a year to get to know a person and build trust in the relationship.[13] Consequently, during the first six months, everyone involved with the alliance has to pay keen attention to each single interaction, both individual and organizational.

Apply Team-Building Processes

Core members of the alliance do not need to go out and climb trees or do other outdoor team-building exercises, although these activities do have value. However, in most cases, there is not enough opportunity to examine relationships and have open discussions about communication. At this point it is important to *build team development approaches into every aspect of the alliance.* (See Chapter Five.)

When a team is created, the following four steps are often experienced, according to Bruce W. Tuckman, an OD trailblazer:[14]

1. *Forming:* The group is getting together. Task-oriented people are trying to work out the group's purpose. Maintenance-oriented people are testing the water, exploring what behavior is allowed. They try to establish a common group aim.
2. *Storming:* Conflict breaks out. Task-oriented people react emotionally to the demands of the task as they see it and attempt to structure the group in pursuit of different goals. Maintenance-oriented people try to sponsor conflicting rules of behavior. They discuss and argue about who takes on each role.
3. *Norming:* The group starts to focus on an agreed view of its own purpose. The initial task leaders have emerged and are sharing information openly. The group develops a sense of cohesion as the maintenance function becomes established.
4. *Performing:* In this final stage of development, the group is working well. Task and maintenance roles are in balance. There is agreement on how the task should be tackled, and solutions start to emerge.

Nicola Phillips believes that an international team usually takes more time for forming, storming, and norming, "because there is so much diversity in terms of perspectives and values within the group."[15] Because of time constraints, many companies rush into the fourth stage with the assumption that they have done the storming and norming and that they can now perform. But what they did for storming and norming was actually no more than an illusion.

Apply Cross-Cultural Meeting Management

Many hours of meetings are required to communicate strategic intent and have it manifested in daily operations. Each meeting attended by bicultural participants has to be conducted in a specific way. A facilitator is needed who has expertise in bicultural or multicultural facilitation. The key here is to use each meeting as an opportunity to practice the five core competencies and the seven mental disciplines. This process not only enhances the productivity of meetings but also fosters the internalization of cross-cultural management skills.

Monitor the Process and Provide Feedback to Each Other

As we saw in the successful alliance management case above, it is important to monitor all aspects of the alliance. It is also important for the two parties to exchange feedback with each other. In the cross-cultural situation, this function requires a combination of sensitivity and accuracy. Having qualified third-party people available is one practical solution.

Clarify Roles and Terms

Role clarification is a common step in any team activity. However, in cross-cultural alliances, terms and language also require thorough clarification. When Dai-ichi Bank and Nippon Kangyo Bank combined to form the Dai-ichi Kangyo Bank, a team of managers from both sides had to publish a two-hundred-word glossary explaining what each bank meant when using exactly the same words.[16] They even had to list such a simple word as *loan* because of differences in interpretation, even though they were both Japanese banks and all team members were Japanese. Thus we can imagine the need for term clarification in cross-cultural alliances. We cannot assume that the Japan contingent understands what we mean because they use Japanized English words, such as *bajitto* for "budget" or *komittomento* for "commitment." I remember a question from a Japanese manager to his American counterpart at a term-clarification session: "Could you explain *the procedure of changing commitment?*"

Acknowledge the Ongoing Process

Remember, we cannot change a culture; rather, a culture changes itself. Creating a new organizational culture takes time. In the case of acquisitions, three to five years is a minimum time period for any alliance. Therefore, an ongoing alignment of the entire operation is required. Although we cannot change a culture, we can facilitate the development of its identity.[17]

All of these points apply to both *gaishi* and *nikkei kigyo*. In fact, these steps provide a very effective method for any cross-cultural organization. A goal is to be able to transform the statement from the beginning of this chapter—"We came from two disparate corporate cultures"—so that it says—"We came from two disparate corporate cultures and forged a stronger one built on the foundation of the best qualities of each."

Moving Forward Across Cultures

Part Four

Moving Forward
Across Cultures

Chapter Thirteen

Embracing Bridge Persons

> *While I'm here in Japan, there is no reason for me not to study Japanese language and culture. Not only does it help my business. More than that, I enjoy the process of learning the unknown.*
> AN AMERICAN EXPATRIATE

Commodore Matthew Perry and the Black Ship are often used as metaphors for the U.S.–Japan business relationship today as American companies enter the Japanese market. In 1853 Commodore Perry arrived at Uraga on the Black Ship. About ten years later, the peace and amity treaty between the United States and Japan (the Kanagawa Treaty) signified the end of Japan's national isolation policy, which had been in place since 1633. Within fifteen years, Japan experienced one of its major historical turning points: the end of the Tokugawa era and the beginning of the Meiji Restoration. Behind the spotlight of the historical events, two Japanese made remarkable contributions to the relationship between the two countries: Nakahama Manjiro (known as John Manjiro) and Joseph Hiko (known as America Hikozo). Neither of them were from samurai families; they were both commoners. Quite by accident, each made a unique contribution as a bridge person between the two countries.

The story of Manjiro is well known among Japanese.[1] When he was fourteen years old, his ship was wrecked, and he was rescued by an American whale-hunting ship. William Whitfield, the captain of the boat, brought Manjiro back to his home town of Fairhaven, Massachusetts, and adopted him as his son. Manjiro then became

177

the first Japanese student to stay with an American family and study in American schools. In 1851, having stayed in the United States for ten years, he returned to Japan. In those days, because of the policy of isolation, he had to undergo a strict interrogation by local officials on Okinawa Island, where he landed. His unique experience and knowledge of the United States caught the attention of those who were trying to open Japan to the world and modernize the country. He began to share his knowledge of technologies such as the steam engine locomotive and new communication systems, which were not available in Japan. In this way, he became a knowledgeable cross-cultural resource person. He was the chief deck officer of the ship *Kairinmaru*, which took a team of samurai to the United States for the Edo government. The *Kairinmaru* team included many players in the Meiji Restoration and are considered to be "Pilgrim Fathers" in Japan. Manjiro also compiled the first English textbook.

Hikozo's story is similar to Manjiro's. In 1850, when he was thirteen years old, Hikozo was rescued by an American ship after drifting for fifty-one days in the Pacific Ocean. He was taken in by Beverly Sanders and was the first Japanese to obtain U.S. citizenship. He worked as an interpreter for the U.S. government and served as an interpreter for the Kanagawa consulate. Hikozo met three U.S. presidents—Franklin Pierce, James Buchanan, and Abraham Lincoln. After the Meiji Restoration, one of his most notable contributions was to bring the philosophy of democracy to Japan.

Other Japanese acted as key bridge persons in the early days of the relationship between the United States and Japan. However, the contributions of John Manjiro and Joseph Hiko are so distinguished that their stories have passed from generation to generation. They were the first cross-cultural consultants between Japan and the United States.

Developing Bridge Persons

The stories of John Manjiro and Joseph Hiko give us practical lessons for developing bridge persons in today's cross-cultural organizations. The first lesson is to have a high level of *commitment*. It is not too difficult to imagine how grateful they were when they were rescued. This gratitude or appreciation became the driving force of their learning. In addition, when they decided to return to Japan, both Manjiro and Hikozo had to prepare themselves for the worst. During that time, there was a rumor that, because of Japan's isolation policies, those who had been rescued by foreign ships would be killed if they returned to Japan. Manjiro had discovered that this rumor was not true while he was in the United States. But he still had risks to face. Hikozo returned to Japan as a U.S. citizen and had to prepare himself for stigma and harassment. These life-and-death experiences strengthened their commitment to work as bridge persons between the two countries.

The second lesson is to acknowledge *support*. Manjiro and Hikozo received different kinds of support. Considering the historical context (the United States wanted to open diplomatic and commercial contacts with Japan, while Japan was caught in the dilemma of deciding whether to modernize or to keep its traditional system), some Japanese and Americans might have tried to use them for their own interests. However, what made the two of them notable bridge persons was the sincere support and help of many people, especially Whitfield and Sanders, the Americans who adopted them.

The third lesson is to achieve *empowerment*. After proving his special expertise, Manjiro was promoted to the status of samurai, which was the highest of the four classes in Japanese society (samurai, farmer, craftsperson, and merchant). In that time, people kept their rank for life; those who were born farmers were farmers their whole life. Manjiro's promotion was a much quicker and bolder decision than those made by some of today's conventional companies. Hikozo also had many opportunities to use his bilingual and bicultural talents.

The fourth lesson is to employ *screening*. Manjiro's and Hikozo's level of commitment and the support they received reinforced their learning abilities. There were quite a few other Japanese who could have been as important as Manjiro and Hikozo. But what differentiated these two from other Japanese who had also been rescued by U.S. boats were their learning abilities. They not only learned English rapidly but also gained an understanding of many processes and ideas, from political systems to the mechanics of the steam engine. Whitfield and Sanders and the others who helped them had the insight to see that their ability to learn far surpassed that of other Japanese they encountered. A keen insight helps in screening the learning potential of individuals. Today's human resources divisions have much more information about the potential of each candidate for the job of bridge person and global manager.

Considering the fact that approximately 240,000 Americans visit Japan each year and 550,000 Japanese visit the United States,[2] it may not be fair to compare today's businesspeople with Manjiro and Hikozo. However, because of the difficulties and complexities of cross-cultural organizations today, in order to bridge the gap between the United States and Japan and to build truly global organizations, we need to remind ourselves of the level of commitment and motivation that Manjiro and Hikozo had over a century ago.

The "Dances with Wolves" Syndrome

In the movie *Dances with Wolves*, I strongly related to the challenge and pathos of the role of bridge person played by Kevin Costner. In the movie, he was a cavalryman assigned to a post in the American West where he encountered Native American tribes. Out of curiosity he became friends with them and started learning their language and culture. When he returned to his own culture he was ostracized and punished. This pattern is very similar to the experience of some expatriates. Those who can appreciate the host country's culture and get excited about their new learning are not always welcomed back by headquarters and their colleagues. This applies in both Japanese and American companies. When I told one expatriate working for an American corporation in Japan how much I was moved by the film because it had captured my personal experience, he said that he felt exactly the same way.

Just as organizations that are aiming to become global companies have to integrate the dilemmas posed by the tension between headquarters and the local operation, so each individual bridge person has to face the same dichotomy. It is not too much to say that the eternal question for a bridge person is whether to choose the home or host country. As long as the majority of headquarters staff maintain an ethnocentric myopia, the agony of the bridge person who appreciates the local culture will continue. In addition, bridge persons have to know how easily people are threatened by and feel insecure around someone who knows more than they do. In fact, Manjiro experienced some harassment from the other

Japanese when he was on the ship *Kairinmaru* as they were crossing the Pacific Ocean. Although bridge persons do not intend to show off their skills and learning, they have to be sensitive to the way they are perceived by their compatriots. This stigma toward bridge persons quite often causes them to reject their home country and reinforces the "Dances with Wolves" syndrome. Studies show this clearly. Approximately 20 percent of U.S. managers quit their company within one year of repatriation.[3] While only 11 percent of Americans, 10 percent of Japanese, and 25 percent of Finns receive promotions after returning home, 77 percent of Americans, 43 percent of Japanese, and 54 percent of Finns are actually demoted.[4] Ironically, those who neither appreciate the host culture nor learn about local operations have no reentry problems (see Figure 13.1).

Figure 13.1. The Challenge for Bridge Persons.

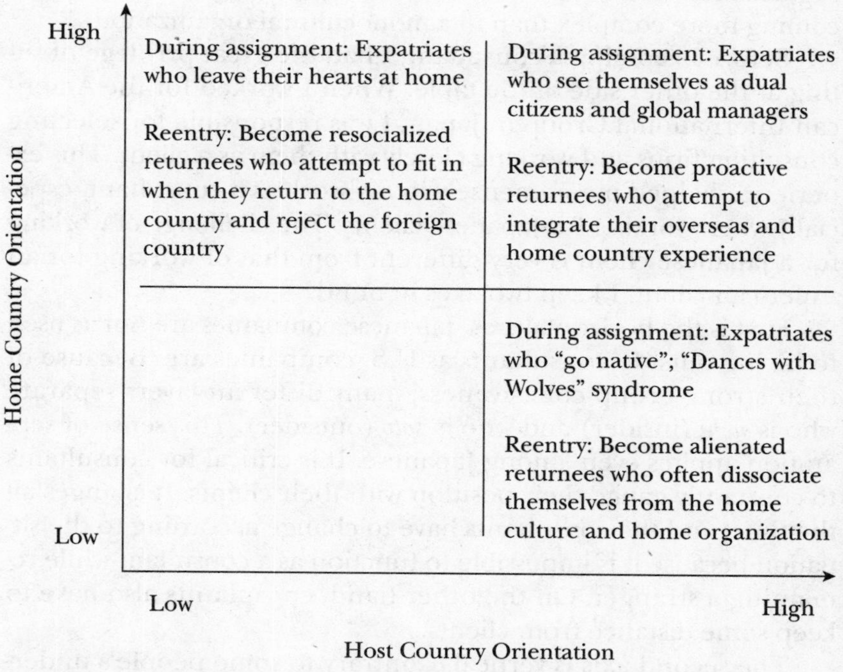

	Low Host Country Orientation	High Host Country Orientation
High Home Country Orientation	During assignment: Expatriates who leave their hearts at home Reentry: Become resocialized returnees who attempt to fit in when they return to the home country and reject the foreign country	During assignment: Expatriates who see themselves as dual citizens and global managers Reentry: Become proactive returnees who attempt to integrate their overseas and home country experience
Low Home Country Orientation		During assignment: Expatriates who "go native"; "Dances with Wolves" syndrome Reentry: Become alienated returnees who often dissociate themselves from the home culture and home organization

Source: Adapted from N. J. Adler, *International Dimensions of Organizational Behavior* (Boston: Kent, 1991).

In order to manage the dichotomy, bridge persons have to practice the mental discipline of style shifting according to the situation. Once again we can see that style shifting is one of the key disciplines that global managers need (see Chapter Six). As we saw in the stories of Manjiro and Hikozo, the benefit of having successful bridge persons is immense for organizations and nations. If the company wants to become a truly global organization, it must commit to embracing bridge persons.

Walking the Tightrope: The Role of Consultant

There is another professional who acts as a bridge person in helping cross-cultural organizations transform themselves into global geocentric corporations: the consultant. As we have seen, because of the increasing demand for different kinds of organizational intervention and cross-cultural process facilitation, consultants are also facing a new challenge. The role of the consultant in a cross-cultural organization, whether it is a subsidiary or a strategic alliance, is becoming more complex than in a monocultural organization.

Before becoming a consultant, I had the great privilege of sitting at the other side of the table. When I worked for the American International Group in Japan, I was responsible for selecting consulting firms and working closely with them as a client. This experience helped me immensely in my work as a consultant, especially when working for Japanese clients. The challenge of working for a Japanese client is very different from that of working for an American client. I keep two axes in mind.

First is the horizontal axis. Japanese companies are not as used to hiring outside consultants as U.S. companies are. Because of their strong group cohesiveness, many different layers separate who is *uchi* (insider) and who is *soto* (outsider). This sense of separation applies even among Japanese. It is critical for consultants to constantly gauge their position with their clients. It changes all the time, and the consultants have to change according to the situation because it is impossible to function as a consultant while remaining a stranger. On the other hand, consultants also have to keep some distance from clients.

The second axis is vertical. Contrary to some people's understanding of the Japanese hierarchical structure, there is no single criterion for measuring who is high and who is low. It depends on the situation, the context. Key variables include age, power position, and other relationships. The priorities of these variables change. From the client's position, consultants are basically vendors. However, the consultant is sometimes called *sensei*—like a teacher or a doctor. If the consultant takes the title of *sensei* for granted and forgets that he or she is a vendor, that is a major mistake. This issue is even more important if the consultant is younger than the clients.

The consultant who pays attention to his or her position on both axes can still do a professional job and avoid being used by one side to blame the other. Unfortunately, this is a common trap for cross-cultural consultants. In many cases, one side tries to influence the other by using the consultant. Building a relationship with a client does not necessarily mean losing neutrality. A consultant who works for a cross-cultural organization has to provide feedback equally to both parties in order to transform cultural conflict into creative cultural synergy.

For consultants working in a bilingual situation, for example, in Japanese and English, there is another pitfall—the use of language. Ideally, a consultant working for a U.S.–Japan cross-cultural business organization should speak both languages. When we speak a different language, we have to shift styles. We cannot speak Japanese with an English-speaking mindset, especially when working for Japanese clients. This issue has another subtle, yet important, aspect for Japanese consultants. English-speaking Japanese are constantly in danger of being stigmatized by other, biased Japanese (see the issue of *eigoya* in Chapter Ten). I intentionally do style reshifting when I work with Japanese clients in order to prove my "Japaneseness" to them. Working with both sides at the same time, as when I facilitate a cross-cultural meeting, is a real challenge. I have to ask participants to style-shift; that is, I request Americans to be patient and not interrupt and Japanese to speak out and not be so quiet. When I do this, I change not only the way I speak to each side, but also my total physiology. One Japanese client in a cross-cultural business-planning meeting that I facilitated said to me after the meeting, "Funakawa-san, you are the first Japanese I have met who is from a U.S. business school yet is still a real Japanese person." I figured out that he was strongly skeptical of Japanese consultants who are graduates of American business schools.

Another skill required for consultants who work for cross-cultural organizations is *role shifting*. There are eight roles for OD consultants: advocate, technical specialist, trainer or educator, collaborator (in problem solving), alternative identifier, fact finder, process specialist, and reflector.[5] Role shifting consists of switching roles according to the situation. In addition, with Japanese clients, vendor and *sensei* need to be added to the repertoire of roles. Cross-cultural consultants working for U.S.–Japan organizations have to stay in a neutral position, on neither the Japanese nor the American side. They must style-shift according to the situation and practice what they preach to clients. At the same time, they have to role-shift according to the situation. It is like walking on a tightrope.

As companies evolve toward being global geocentric organizations, the role of the bridge person becomes invaluable. We should remember that a bridge person is not born but is made by organizational support and by the strong commitment of a person who is willing to take on the burden and joy of crossing cultures.

Chapter Fourteen

Searching for a New Identity for the 21st Century

> *If we have only one response to each situation, we become*
> *a robot. If we have two choices for every situation, we have*
> *a dilemma. When we have three responses, that is the*
> *beginning of flexibility. If we realize that we have infinite*
> *possibilities in any given situation, we become totally free.*
> DEEPAK CHOPRA[1]

In this concluding chapter, I explore future directions for transcultural management.

The Challenge of the Borderful World

When the Berlin wall disappeared, symbolizing the end of the Cold War, many believed that a global, borderless world was becoming a reality. People declared the triumph of capitalism. Multinational corporations seemed to be entering their golden age. But what we are now seeing differs from these expectations. The *Wall Street Journal* focused on this global paradox:[2]

> Following World War II, many predicted that a global economy and global communications would lead to a world-wide community. Nationalism, they said, would decline as ever more people saw us all as passengers on lifeboat Earth.
>
> But the growth of the global economy and of more powerful transitional institutions is producing the opposite effect. Instead

of fading away, nationalism is flourishing, and not just in the war-ravaged Balkans. Now even tiny groups of people can contemplate breaking away from the world economy on their own. Regions nursing ancient grievances are claiming independence, or at least autonomy, confident they aren't committing economic suicide. At the same time, the big corporations and institutions shaping the world economy seem so remote that many people turn to local ethnic groups and obscure languages for their identity, furthering the world's political fragmentation.

Hiroyuki Itami, a professor at Hitotsubashi University, described this phenomenon as "the borderful world." He said, "From the viewpoint of the long-term trend—such as one or two hundred years—it is clear that the world economy is moving toward the borderless. However, we will see a sort of swing of the pendulum against too much movement toward the borderless in the last ten to fifteen years. Although their economic activities go beyond borders, it is important for corporations to be very aware of borders in this borderful world."[3] Like others, Itami explained that the reason for this emerging borderful world is the collapse of the two superpowers—the United States and the USSR. Together they created a lid like that on a pressure cooker, which suppressed ethnicity and nationalism. In the early 1980s, John Naisbitt predicted in his book, *Megatrends,* that the globalization of our economies would trigger a new linguistic and cultural assertiveness.[4] This emerging multilingual, multicultural, and multinational environment challenges multinational corporations.

There seems to be a gap between what is written about global companies and what is actually happening in these organizations. Scholars tend to idealize successful companies. A survey held by Gemini Consulting and the International Consortium for Executive Development Research unveiled this gap. After examining the international competitive capabilities of twelve leading multinational companies, they concluded that the world's leading multinationals are actually far less global-minded than they think they are. Most companies place little emphasis on such issues as managing a culturally diverse workforce, managing cross-border alliances, transnational teams, and international assignments.[5] The reality of managing a multilingual, multicultural, and multinational organization is much more difficult than was once thought. An article in *The Economist* described this arduous task:[6]

"There are very few multicultural multinationals; the truly global multicultural company does not yet exist."
DAVID DE PURY, CO-CHAIRMAN OF ASEA BROWN BOVERI

This dismissal is the more striking coming from ABB, a firm with a board of eight directors from four different nationalities; an executive committee of eight people from five countries; English as its corporate language; and financial results reported in dollars. Perhaps only Royal Dutch/Shell—another European giant of mixed parentage, which has some 38 nationalities in its London head office—can claim to have advanced so far down the multicultural route. What chance is there then for big American or Japanese firms that think globalization simply means having an occasional board meeting in London or Paris?

How many Japanese and U.S. companies can respond to this question? Not many. In the age of a "renaissance in language and cultural assertiveness,"[7] a multinational corporation (MNC) has to become a "triple M"NC (a multilingual, multicultural, and multinational corporation). This is the toughest challenge an MNC faces.

Beyond Diversity Programs

Although the United States and Japan are culturally very different, both have the same cross-cultural disability. Neither is used to managing "triple-M" organizations. Some Americans may say, "But the United States is the most culturally diverse country in the world. We know how to handle diversity. We have cultural diversity programs." Many American companies are far ahead of Japanese companies in terms of their awareness of cultural issues and their experience in managing diversity. However, companies that introduce diversity programs don't always have a clear understanding of what it means to manage diversity. In many cases, managers take a diversity-training program only to appear politically correct. A survey of over three hundred companies in New York (one of the most diverse cities in the world) shows that they are doing what is necessary to comply with government employment law and little more.[8] The *New York Times* pointed out, "For the most part they have not taken the step beyond what would move diversity out of a pigeon hole in the personnel department and into the strategic center of the corporate environment."[9] In addition, as we have seen, American management tends to underestimate national cultural differences and overestimate universal rights. An internally heterogeneous society creates this cultural blind spot for the United States, while Japanese homogeneity has not taught Japan how to manage cultural differences.

In this sense, European companies are a little more advanced because they have lived in a triple-M environment. The fact that multicultural management seminars containing systematic cross-cultural management research data (such as Hofstede's model and Trompenaars's work) have caught the attention of executives in Europe more than in Japan or in the United States shows their keen awareness and sense of urgency.[10] Japanese and American managers tend to say, "Sure, there are many countries in Europe. But there are fewer time-zone differences. They are basically the same." Many Europeans say, "You think that Europe is just one unit. But each country is very different." Even among Scandinavian countries, the Norwegians are different from the Swedes and the Danes. Again, each country has its uniqueness and we cannot generalize about cultural traits. No wonder that many companies setting up systems in Europe assume regional similarity, then are surprised to find cultural gaps within the region.

Valuing diversity is indispensable in the emerging triple-M environment, but it is a prodigious task. It involves a shift from the Golden Rule—treat others as you wish them to treat you—to the so-called Platinum Rule—treat others as they wish to be treated.[11] It requires people to relinquish assumptions about the universal rightness of their own values. This letting go of our own assumptions contains a subtle but profound insight into what it really means to transcend cultural differences. Assumptions include not only our stereotypes and preconceived notions but also cultural knowledge itself. Since we have discussed many reasons to develop awareness of and sensitivity to other cultures, this may sound contradictory. Also, letting go of our assumptions challenges our identities and makes us feel uncomfortable. But we do not have to worry.

A Super-Synthesized Model: The Story of an Old Cat

A few Japanese and American managers I have met have learned all the key skills of cross-cultural management from their own experiences. They say, "In the end, there aren't any important management differences between Japan and the United States. Just pay attention to basics and you'll do fine." As we have seen, we have to be careful of such statements. However, although it may seem to contradict what I have said so far, some people are truly entitled to make such claims. They may have reached a point where they no longer need to consciously practice such transcultural skills as style shifting. On the surface they may appear clueless and incompetent in intercultural business environments, but there is a difference. It is similar to other phenomena that we think we can see. For instance, a snapshot of a gyroscope makes it appear motionless. A highly experienced martial artist does not look tough. In the martial arts, it is not until someone says "I did not realize that you were a martial artist" that you can consider yourself no longer a beginner. An old martial arts story explains this clearly:[12]

> Once there was a samurai who lived in a town. One day a big, old rat came into his house and, try as he might, the samurai could not get rid of it. He threatened the rat and set traps, but to no avail. The rat always eluded him and his traps and stayed on in his house.
>
> The samurai decided to try using a cat to catch the rat. He heard of a famous black cat who came from a long line of fighting cats and had a high reputation for his technical ability. So he borrowed this cat and set it down in his house to catch the rat. Despite his great technical ability, the black cat could not catch the big, old rat.
>
> The samurai was disappointed but heard of another cat with a high reputation for his fighting spirit and strong presence. This was a tiger-striped cat and also came from excellent fighting parentage. So he placed the tiger-striped cat in his house and waited. But like the black cat before him, the tiger-striped cat failed to catch the big, old rat.
>
> The samurai was upset. Two good ratters had failed to catch the big, old rat. But then he heard of a third cat, ash-gray in color. This one had a high reputation for being calm and centered and having great self-confidence. His lineage was excellent. The samurai hoped that at last he had found the cat to catch his rat. So he put the ash-gray cat in his house and left it to catch the rat. But just as with the black cat and the tiger-striped cat before him, the ash-gray cat could not manage to catch the big, old rat.
>
> Angry and despairing, the samurai attacked the rat himself with his sword. But the big, old rat was extremely skillful and avoided

the samurai's sword like a butterfly! The samurai cut thin air. The rat was just like an acrobat and eventually humiliated the samurai by giving him a sharp bite.

The samurai was beginning to resign himself to having to live with the big, old rat in his house as a permanent guest when he heard a rumor of another cat famed for catching rats. The samurai made inquiries and decided to borrow the cat and have one last try at catching the rat.

So he took the cat and placed it in his house. However, he did not have too much hope as the cat was very old and scruffy and unassuming. Nevertheless, he left it there.

The old, scruffy cat walked very slowly up to the rat and killed it. The samurai was astounded. That night, the black cat, the tiger-striped cat, and the ash-gray cat all came to talk to the old, scruffy cat, for they were intrigued and mystified by his ability. The samurai hosted the meeting in his living room.

The black cat was the first to speak: "I come from a long line of fighting cats. I learned high technical skills for catching rats from very experienced teachers. I have never failed to catch a rat before. Why did I fail this time?"

The old, scruffy cat answered: "Your technique is excellent. No other cat can match you in technique. But technique, however superb, is not enough to catch such a rat."

Then the tiger-striped cat spoke: "I too believe that good technique is not enough. So I have developed a strong fighting spirit in addition. With a strong fighting spirit I can paralyze a rat just by my look and presence. But not this one. Why?"

The old, scruffy cat replied: "You do indeed have a great deal of courage and fighting spirit. You may think this is enough. But what would you do if you met a rat who had an even stronger fighting spirit? A fighting spirit and courage are not absolute powers."

Lastly the ash-gray cat spoke out: "I agree with you that technique and fighting spirit alone are not sufficient to catch such a rat. So I approach my opponents beyond these two. I aim for a high spiritual level in which I determine to become nothing, to unify myself with nature. This being achieved, I can become myself again but now in freedom. This has never failed in overcoming all my opponents in the past. But with this big, old rat it did not work. I really do not understand why."

The old, scruffy cat said: "Your way is good and you are going in the right direction. But you are too determined to become nothing and to become yourself again. It is this determination which is your weakness. It disturbs and distracts you from true natural union and selfhood."

The black cat, tiger-striped cat, and ash-gray cat then all praised the old, scruffy cat for his skill and wisdom. But the old, scruffy cat stopped them, saying: "In my youth I knew a great, old cat and I watched him very carefully. He did nothing but sleep all day. Yet there were never any rats around. He would be taken to a place where there were lots of rats and they would just leave without him doing anything! I asked him his secret, but he didn't answer. He couldn't answer because he did not have any self-consciousness or pay any attention to rats. He had reached the ultimate stage of transcending fighting. You all praise me for catching this rat. But in truth I am very far away from being like that great, old cat."

At this point, the samurai asked the old cat, "What is the key to the martial arts?"

The old, scruffy cat replied, "Martial arts are not ways to beat others and win. They are disciplines for handling whatever may happen to us without losing ourselves. Therefore, you have to prepare for death without fear. By facing death, you can keep real peace in your mind. If you persist in your own point of view, you will always have enemies. If you insist on right, there is always left, on Yin, there is always Yang. In this way, you will misjudge situations. By letting go, you will be able to respond to any situation, in any environment. Don't think too much. It will come naturally."

The Unlimited Learning Spiral

Confucius wrote about the value of learning something new by revisiting old wisdom.[13] The story of the old cat provides us with more than an esoteric lesson about martial arts. It contains an important message for us about the fundamental principles of learning and development that can be applied to today's business world, including working in the triple-M environment. The three young cats shared their different methods and approaches. The old cat explained the ultimate stage, in which all the methods are synthesized. It is called *mu*. This stage is not merely a compromise or a combination of the different values. *Mu* means nothingness, but it is a nothingness that contains everything.

Kitaro Nishida, a Japanese philosopher in the Meiji era, provided a good explanation of this process, linking it to Western philosophy, especially to Hegelian theory. According to Nishida, to make this synthesis possible requires a field where we can transcend all the contradictions between thesis and antithesis. He called this field absolute nothingness, which is the same as *mu*.[14] Achieving *mu* is one of the goals of Zen practice and it is often described by martial artists, fine artists, and other professionals as a level they reach after much strict training and practice. Although many Westerners think that *mu* is particular to Zen or to other Oriental disciplines, it actually is the same concept as love—not romantic love, but love in the sense of agape. In fact, Master Ueshiba, the founder of aikido, a form of martial arts, said that he reached a stage that he called love.

I had some qualms about using the concepts of *mu* and agape in this book because many people have biased reactions to these terms. I do not want to make this into a quasispiritual text. But remember that this is a time when new business paradigms have become very important. Just as martial artists reached the stage of *mu* and agape through real life-and-death combat situations, so we are able to reach it through our practice of business. Senge also mentioned this process in relation to the learning organization:[15]

> If openness is a quality of relationships, then building relationships characterized by openness may be one of the most high-leverage actions to build organizations characterized by openness. This is precisely what I and many of my colleagues have observed time and again—that "learningful" relationships among key members of the organization have an extraordinary impact on the larger organization. When small groups of people (as few as two or three) become deeply committed and open they create a microcosm of a learning organization. This microcosm not only teaches them the skills they need but becomes a model for others.
>
> The impulse toward openness, as O'Brien says, "is the spirit of love." Love is, of course, a difficult word to use in the context of business and management. But O'Brien does not mean romantic love. In fact, the type of love that underlies openness, what the Greeks called agape, has little to do with emotions. It has everything to do with intentions—commitment to serve one another, and willingness to be vulnerable in the context of that service. The

best definition of the love that underlies openness is the full and unconditional commitment to another's "completion," to another being all that she or he can and wants to be.

Gary Hamel and C. K. Prahalad wrote, "Creating a learning organization is only half the solution. Just as important is creating an unlearning organization. Unlearning is removing defective genes."[16] Those who understand this statement may see the reason why we are talking about *mu* and agape in the context of business. They have the opportunity to join the journey—the journey of the unlimited learning spiral (Figure 14.1).

The participants in this journey know that learning is discovering our own ignorance. (Both Confucius and Socrates said that real knowledge is learning ignorance.) They experience joy and excitement when facing the unknown. They make themselves completely open, which leads to *mu* and agape. At this point, opposing values no longer contradict each other. This is a full nothingness, a nothingness full of infinite possibilities. In this sense, zero is equal to the infinite ($0 = \infty$). Here, as Nishida said, knowledge is love and love is knowledge.[17]

Not many of us reach this stage. Instead, we are caught in the trap of limited learning, which causes us to fear new discoveries

Figure 14.1. The Unlimited Learning Spiral.

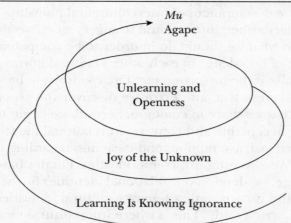

and the unknown. We feel insecure. We may be able to learn to a certain extent, but we cannot go all the way because we cannot unlearn. We are bothered by contradictions and dilemmas. As Hamel and Prahalad showed, small children can learn quickly because of their ability to unlearn.[18] Interestingly enough, small children (especially infants) from different cultures can play with each other without feeling cultural conflict. They don't have any preconceived notions. I'm amazed that my fifteen-month-old son has no sense of fear of the unknown and can learn so quickly. When we were babies, all of us were participants in the unlimited learning spiral.

Nishida stated that pure experience does not separate subject and object, or knowledge and experience. This is the supreme experience.[19] All of us once had this experience. As we grow and develop our identities, it gets more difficult to stay in the unlimited learning spiral. In order to bring ourselves back on track, we have to handle identity issues. Cross-cultural work situations in the global business environment constantly challenge our identities. The identity issue is a critical matter to each of us. We need to search for new identities in this new era.

Transcultural Competency as the Identity of the Global Citizen

In their identity management theory, Tadasu Imahori and William Cupach, experts in intercultural communication, describe three stages in the development of intercultural relationships and competency.[20] First, when intercultural strangers meet, we are not able to agree on what we should do in order to be competent because of our lack of knowledge of each other's cultural norms and rules. Paradoxically, by being incompetent we can learn to become competent. Through trial and error we discover the aspects of our identities that we share in common. Second, we begin to develop a mutually acceptable and convergent relational identity. We develop shared tacit assumptions and meanings regarding the nature of reality. We also establish common rules. Finally, based on the second stage, we develop our relational identities further by renegotiating and incorporating separate cultural identities. As Imahori and Cupach said, "This is where intercultural relationships realize the potential to evolve into interpersonal relationships."[21]

However, they also note that many people cannot reach the third stage and so have no chance of renegotiating their own identities.[22]

This process is applicable in the corporate world. As we have seen, many corporate alliances give up before establishing new relational identities and therefore do not have the opportunity to renegotiate. Developing transcultural competency requires us to transform our own identities.

In today's interconnected and interdependent business world, we have to constantly renegotiate our own identities. Imahori and Cupach give us an important message:[23]

> Indeed, the more two individuals interact and become interdependent, the more complex their relationship becomes and, therefore, the more aspects of identity will have to be negotiated and renegotiated.

We are now searching for new identities, both individual and organizational. First of all, we must start negotiating and renegotiating our own ethnocentrism, which is ultimately the same as egocentrism. The five core transcultural competencies and the seven mental disciplines contain the techniques for transforming ourselves if we accept and practice them. The new identity of "global citizen" requires transcultural competency. We don't have to be afraid of transformation as long as we know that the metamorphosed identity will be different from the way we are now, in the sense that it is a larger or more real self.

We have just started learning about our new environment. From an ethnocentric view, the emerging multilingual, multicultural, and multinational environment may seem to reflect a fragmented world, as if the world is falling apart. But from a global geocentric perspective, the world is actually regaining its original identity as the field of infinite possibilities. It is our decision which to choose.

Interventions for Transcultural Organizations

Although there is no single generic solution applicable to a specific situation for each organization, the following two examples outline transcultural organizational intervention.

Case 1: Global Workshop Conference

Situation

The Japan branch of an American company sponsored a global workshop, inviting forty managers from the United States and eleven Asia-Pacific countries including Singapore, Indonesia, and Australia.

Objective

To assist the Japan branch, the U.S. headquarters, and participants from the Asia-Pacific region to build work as a transcultural team. This program served:

1. To teach the key framework of transcultural management and to practice the five core transcultural competencies and seven mental disciplines as a team
2. To develop the geocentric mindset, reflecting upon each national mindset (that is, core values, norms, and belief systems)
3. To align the geocentric mindset with the company's Asian and global corporate missions and values

Program Outline and Main Topics

Preconference Workshop for Japanese Managers (Two Days)

This session was provided for Japanese managers in the Japanese language to maximize the effectiveness of the workshop by:

1. Encouraging the Japanese managers to overcome their reticent attitudes and to participate actively in the workshop
2. Reviewing key transcultural management concepts in the Japanese language so that they could familiarize themselves with content (the actual workshop was held in English)
3. Ensuring the logical and critical thinking that is lacking in the Japanese educational system

Main Topics of the Workshop

1. Introduction to transcultural management: stages of globalization, nature of multicultural organizations, ascribed context and achieved content, multidimensional cross-cultural research
2. Logical and critical thinking: deductive, inductive, and abductive thinking, grouping and ranking, problem solving, logic tree, hypothesis test
3. Preview of the program: introduction of fundamental team management concepts, including leadership, conflict resolution, and meetings management

Outline of the Global Workshop

Day 1: Transcultural Management

Participants developed an understanding of the key issues of multicultural organizations. They explored ways to deal with managing an effective transnational corporation. Contents covered were:

1. The five transcultural competencies
2. The seven mental disciplines
3. Multicultural meetings management
4. Case: transferring knowledge in a multicultural organization

Day 2 (A.M.): Creating a National Mindset

Participants created their own national mindset (that is, the core values, norms, and belief systems of a specific country or culture), such as a Japanese mindset, an American mindset, and a Malaysian mindset, so that they could share and become sensitized to each other's cultural values (see Chapter Five).

Day 2 (P.M.): Creating the Current Corporate Mindset
Participants were divided into six groups by mixed nationality and created the current corporate mindset. Each group discussed the following questions:

1. What are the core values that we are providing through our products and services?
2. What are the critical incidents that influence our worldwide operation? List them and consider their implications for management behavior and thought patterns.
3. What are the unique work styles in our organization? List what you realized when you joined our organization.
4. What kind of norms and assumed rules did we realize?
5. What kind of skills do we value in our organization?
6. What are the underlying assumptions that developed our missions and strategies?
7. Based on the above questions, what are the current corporate mindsets?

Day 3: Creating the Geocentric Global Mindset
Sensitizing the outcome of Day 2 (the national mindset and the current mindset), participants developed the global geocentric corporate mindset. Group discussion was based on the following questions and issues:

1. What are the key values and beliefs that we learned from each national mindset?
2. Identify potential drawbacks in the current corporate mindsets in the context of the multicultural organization.
3. Identify key strengths in the current corporate mindsets in the context of a multicultural organization.
4. How should we change any disempowering beliefs and values, if any?
5. Based on the above questions and issues, what should we possess as global geocentric mindsets?

Case 2: Organizational Learning and Development Project for a Cross-Border Joint Venture

Situation

The Japanese branch of an American company planning to acquire a Japanese company was aware of the triple culture gap (see Chapter Twelve).

Objective

To align two different corporate mindsets (the *gaishi* and the Japanese company) with the strategic intent of the new organization. This project was conducted:

1. To build a shared understanding of each other's strategic intent for the new organization
2. To identify and improve understanding of critical success factors for the project
3. To clarify the current corporate mindsets (that is, the core values, norms, and belief systems) of the *gaishi* and the Japanese partner in order to identify each other's assumptions, perceptions, and expectations of the new styles and norms of the new organization
4. To create a new corporate mindset and new guiding principles, including critical areas of organizational management such as decision making, information sharing, communication, and performance appraisal
5. To identify potential areas of conflict and to strategize ways to mediate

Process

Phase I: Binational or Bicultural Interview Research

This consisted of interview-based research for the *gaishi* and the partner.

Phase II: Joint Strategizing Session

Upon analyzing the Phase I interview research, the steering committee (a joint team of the *gaishi* and the Japanese company) for the project and a team of Globis consultants strategized Phase III program implementation by:

1. Identifying areas on which to focus
2. Prioritizing expected outcomes
3. Finalizing the schedule
4. Identifying participants

Phase III: Program Implementation (Tentative)

Step 1: A Two-Day, Off-Site Session for American Management in the Gaishi (Languages: English and Japanese)

Step 2: A Two-Day, Off-Site Session for the Japanese (Language: Japanese)
The contents of the two sessions were identical:

1. Understanding the core framework of the joint venture management by using cases
2. Identifying the current corporate mindset, including history, work styles, the nature of services and products, and values and beliefs
3. Envisioning the partner's corporate mindset

Step 3: A Two-Day Joint Program (Languages: Japanese and English)
Based on the outcomes of Steps 1 and 2, Step 3 invited both contingents. The outcomes of this session were a set of guiding principles and the new mindset of the organization.

Glossary

As has been discussed, the Japanese language is very high-context. The following translations are based on the context of this book. There are many different meanings and translations for each word.

bucho: Division or department manager

bucho dairi: Assistant division or department manager

bun: Role

dojo: A place for both physical and spiritual training of martial arts and Zen

doki: Same year of entering a school or organization

enryo: Holding back, reticent

gaijin: Foreigner

gaishi: Foreign capital (company)

hito: People

honne: De facto, real intention

ichibu jyo-jyo kaisha: Companies listed in the Tokyo, Osaka, and Nagoya stock exchange, Section I

jishuku: Self-restraint

kacho: Section manager

kacho dairi: Assistant section manager

kane: Money

kata: Form

keiretsu: Groups of corporations

kokusaika: Internationalization

kouhai: Less experienced, senior member in an organization

ma: Space, timing, and silence

mono: Things, fixed assets

mu: Nothingness, full of nothingness

nemawashi: Lay the groundwork

nikkei kigyo: A Japanese company abroad

senpai: More experienced, senior member of an organization

shunin: Section chief

soto: Outside

tatemae: Public face, surface, facade

uchi: Inside

wa: Harmony

Chapter Notes

Preface

1. Japan Foundation Center for Global Partnership, *Supplying Information and Data on Contemporary Japan to the United States* (Tokyo: Author, 1991), pp. 15–16.
2. K. Hayashi, *Ibunka Interface Keiei* (Intercultural Management) (Tokyo: Nihon Keizai Shinbunsha, 1994), p. 87.

Chapter One

1. S. P. Huntington, "The Clash of Civilizations?" *A Foreign Affairs Reader,* Summer 1993, p. 22.
2. G. Hofstede, *Cultures and Organizations: Software of the Mind* (Maidenhead, Berkshire, U.K.: McGraw-Hill, 1991), p. 181.
3. For example, "Beyond Pearl Harbor: Japan's Choice," *Nikkei* Newspaper (Japanese ed.), November 16, 1991; "Remembering Pearl Harbor," *Newsweek,* November 28, 1991.
4. "Japanese Companies Canceled Their Advertisements," *Nikkei* Newspaper (Japanese ed.), November 27, 1991.
5. N. J. Adler, *International Dimensions of Organizational Behavior* (Boston: Kent, 1991), p. 59.
6. H. Ando, *Nichibei Jyoho Masatsu* (The Information Friction Between the United States and Japan) (Tokyo: Iwanami, 1991).

Chapter Two

1. S. H. Rhinesmith, *A Manager's Guide to Globalization* (Burr Ridge, Ill.: Business One Irwin, 1993), p. 191.
2. N. J. Adler, *International Dimensions of Organizational Behavior* (Boston: Kent, 1991), p. 96.
3. P. R. Harris and R. T. Moran, *Managing Cultural Differences,* 3rd ed. (Houston: Gulf, 1991), pp. 206–211.
4. G. Hofstede, *Cultures and Organizations: Software of the Mind* (Maidenhead, Berkshire, U.K.: McGraw-Hill, 1991), pp. 4–5.
5. G. Fisher, *Mindsets: The Role of Culture and Perception in International Relations* (Yarmouth, Maine: Intercultural Press, 1988).

6. Y. Kensaju, "Ibunkakan Communication to Gengo No Mondai" (Intercultural Communication and Language Issues) in J. Takahashi, O. Nakayama, K. Midooka, and F. Watanage, eds., *Ibunka heno Strategy* (Strategies for Intercultural Issues) (Tokyo: Kawashima, 1991), p. 133.

7. A. Laurent, "Cross-Cultural Puzzle of Global Human Resource Management," in P. Lorange, ed., *Human Resource Management, 25*(1) (Spring 1986), pp. 91–102.

8. J. Condon, *An Introduction to Intercultural Communication* (New York: Bobbs-Merrill, 1975), p. 60.

9. S. P. Huntington, "The Clash of Civilizations?" *A Foreign Affairs Reader,* Summer 1993, pp. 22–49.

10. T. Goss, R. Pascale, and A. Athos, "The Reinvention Roller Coaster: Risking the Present for a Powerful Future," *Harvard Business Review,* November–December 1993, p. 107.

11. "Kuchihateta Soichiro-ism" (Collapse of Soichiro-ism), *Sentaku* (Tokyo: Sentaku Publishing, May 1994), pp. 86–89.

12. Hofstede, *Cultures and Organizations,* p. 183.

13. N. J. Adler and M. Jelinek, "Is 'Organization Culture' Culture Bound?" in P. Lorange, ed., *Human Resource Management, 25*(1) (Spring 1986), p. 84.

14. Hofstede, *Cultures and Organizations,* pp. 182–183.

15. P.-O. Berg, "Organization Change as a Symbolic Transformation Process," in P. J. Frost, ed., *Organizational Culture,* 5th printing (Thousand Oaks, Calif.: Sage, 1985), p. 294.

16. S. C. Schneider, "National Versus Corporate Culture: Implications for Human Resource Management," in P. Lorange, ed., *Human Resource Management, 27*(1) (New York: Wiley, 1986), p. 135.

17. C. Hampden-Turner, "The Boundaries of Business: The Cross-Cultural Quagmire," *Harvard Business Review,* September–October 1991, p. 95.

Chapter Three

1. Translated by Kay M. Jones and Anthony Pan.

Chapter Four

1. G. S. Yip, *Total Global Strategy* (Upper Saddle River, N.J.: Prentice Hall, 1992), p. 207.

2. This model was inspired by the works of many scholars, including H. V. Perlmutter, "The Tortuous Evolution of the Multinational Corporation," in J. C. Baker, J. K. Ryans, Jr., and D. G. Howard, eds., *International Business Classics* (San Francisco: The New Lexington Press,

1988); C. A. Bartlett and S. Ghoshal, *Managing Across Borders: The Transnational Solution* (Boston: Harvard Business School Press, 1989); and R. T. Moran, P. R. Harris, and W. G. Stripp, *Developing the Global Organization* (Houston: Gulf, 1993).

3. Perlmutter, "The Tortuous Evolution of the Multinational Corporation."

4. Perlmutter, "The Tortuous Evolution of the Multinational Corporation," p. 491.

5. Moran, Harris, and Stripp, *Developing the Global Organization.*

6. Moran, Harris, and Stripp, *Developing the Global Organization.*

7. S. H. Robock and K. Simmonds, *International Business and Multinational Enterprises,* 4th ed. (Burr Ridge, Ill.: Irwin, 1989), p. 220.

8. Moran, Harris, and Stripp, *Developing the Global Organization,* p. 127.

9. Robock and Simmonds, *International Business and Multinational Enterprises,* p. 219.

10. Robock and Simmonds, *International Business and Multinational Enterprises,* pp. 219–220.

11. Bartlett and Ghoshal, *Managing Across Borders,* p. 89.

12. Perlmutter, "The Tortuous Evolution of the Multinational Corporation," p. 499.

13. P. R. Harris and R. T. Moran, *Managing Cultural Differences,* 3rd ed. (Houston: Gulf, 1991), p. 302.

14. Harris and Moran, *Managing Cultural Differences,* p. 284.

15. "Companies Use Cross-Cultural Training to Help Their Employees Adjust Abroad," *Wall Street Journal,* August 4, 1992.

16. "International Gurus: Teaching Big Business About Foreign Cultures Is Big Business Itself," *Wall Street Journal,* June 2, 1993.

17. S. B. Odenwald, *Global Training: How to Design a Program for the Multinational Corporation* (Burr Ridge, Ill.: Business One Irwin, 1993), p. 109.

18. N. M. Tichy, "Global Development," in V. Pucik, N. M. Tichy, and C. K. Barnett, eds., *Globalizing Management: Creating and Leading the Competitive Organization* (New York: Wiley, 1992), p. 206.

Chapter Five

1. P.A.L. Evans and Y. Doz, "Dualities: A Paradigm for Human Resource and Organizational Development in Complex Multinationals," in V. Pucik, N. M. Tichy, and C. K. Barnett, eds., *Globalizing Management: Creating and Leading the Competitive Organization* (New York: Wiley, 1992), p. 87.

2. G. Fisher, *Mindsets: The Role of Culture and Perception in International Relations* (Yarmouth, Maine: Intercultural Press, 1988), p. 2.

3. S. H. Rhinesmith, *A Manager's Guide to Globalization* (Burr Ridge, Ill.: Business One Irwin, 1993), p. 24.
4. W. Taylor, "The Logic of Global Business: An Interview with ABB's Percy Banevik," *Harvard Business Review,* March–April 1991, p. 94.
5. There is a good book on this subject: H. Okumura, *Kaisha-Honni Shugi wa Kusureruka?* (Collapse of Corporate-Centrism?) (Tokyo: Iwanami, 1992).
6. S. Hori, *So-gyousha shugi Keiei* (Management Frontiers Facing Japanese Corporations: Second Commencement) (Tokyo: President, 1992), pp. 74–86.
7. Hori, "So-gyousha shugi Keiei," pp. 74–86.
8. Comment by Gregory Ramsey, president of the consulting firm Strategic Analysis of Reading, Pa., in "The Trials of Two Acquirers," *International Business,* February 1995, p. 35.
9. G. Fukushima, *Nichibei Keizai Masatsu No Sejigaku* (Political Study on the U.S.–Japan Economic Friction) (Tokyo: Asahi Shinbunsha, 1992).
10. From a lecture given at the American Graduate School of International Management, February 1991.
11. R. T. Moran, "National Stereotypes: How Far Can You Trust Them?" *International Management,* March 1987, p. 58.
12. R. T. Moran, "A Formula for Success in Multicultural Organizations," *International Management,* December 1988, p. 74.
13. Moran, "National Stereotypes," p. 74.
14. N. J. Adler, *International Dimensions of Organizational Behavior* (Boston: Kent, 1991), p. 126.
15. Adler, *International Dimensions of Organizational Behavior,* p. 128.
16. T. Cox, Jr., *Cultural Diversity in Organizations* (San Francisco: Berrett-Koehler, 1994), p. 214.
17. Moran, "A Formula for Success in Multicultural Organizations," p. 74.
18. R. Moran and P. Harris, *Managing Cultural Synergy* (Houston: Gulf, 1982), pp. 5–6.
19. S. R. Covey, *The 7 Habits of Highly Effective People* (New York: Simon & Schuster, 1989), p. 277.
20. R. T. Moran, P. R. Harris, and W. G. Stripp, *Developing the Global Organization* (Houston: Gulf, 1993), pp. 79–80.
21. W. G. Dyer, *Team Building: Issues and Alternatives* (Reading, Mass.: Addison-Wesley, 1977), p. 91.
22. M. O'Hara-Devereaux and R. Johansen, *Globalwork: Bridging Distance, Culture, and Time* (San Francisco: Jossey-Bass, 1994), p. 122.
23. O'Hara-Devereaux and Johansen, *Globalwork,* p. 134.

24. "Saishin Global Keiei" (The Leading Global Management), *Nikkei Business,* February 26, 1996. p. 23.

Chapter Six

1. M. Ray and R. Myers, *Creativity in Business* (New York: Doubleday, 1986), p. 40.
2. S. Covey, *Principle-Centered Leadership* (New York: Simon & Schuster, 1990), p. 179.
3. P. Senge, *The Fifth Discipline: The Art and Practice of the Learning Organization* (New York: Doubleday Currency, 1990), pp. 10–11.
4. K. Hayashi, *Ibunka Interface Keiei* (Intercultural Management) (Tokyo: Nihon Keizai Shinbunsha, 1994), p. 222.

Chapter Seven

1. G. Fisher, *Mindsets: The Role of Culture and Perception in International Relations* (Yarmouth, Maine: Intercultural Press, 1988), p. 25.
2. A. Webber, "What's So New About the New Economy?" *Harvard Business Review,* January–February 1993, p. 28.
3. Webber, "What's So New About the New Economy?" p. 32.
4. E. T. Hall, *Beyond Culture* (New York: Anchor Books, 1976), pp. 85–103.
5. I was inspired by Hall's model in *Beyond Culture* in developing this model.
6. J. K. Johansson and I. Nonaka, "Market Research the Japanese Way," *Harvard Business Review,* May–June 1987, p. 16.
7. "Japanese Annual Reports: Reading More . . . and Learning Less?" *Electronic Business Asia,* April 1992, pp. 40–48.
8. F. Trompenaars, *Riding the Waves of Culture: Understanding Diversity in Global Business,* rev. ed. (Burn Ridge, Ill.: Irwin Professional Publishing, 1994).
9. Trompenaars, *Riding the Waves of Culture,* pp. 102–105.
10. G. Hofstede, *Cultures and Organizations: Software of the Mind* (Maidenhead, Berkshire, U.K.: McGraw-Hill, 1991), p. 251.
11. Hofstede, *Cultures and Organizations,* p. 13.
12. Hofstede, *Cultures and Organizations,* p. 51.
13. Hofstede, *Cultures and Organizations,* p. 28.
14. Hofstede, *Cultures and Organizations,* p. 113.
15. Hofstede, *Cultures and Organizations,* p. 82.
16. Hofstede, *Cultures and Organizations,* pp. 166–170.
17. J. Fallows, *More Like Us* (Boston: Houghton Mifflin, 1989), p. 47.
18. "Tokushu na Nihonjinn Ishiki Sutete" (Abandoning "the Japanese-Are-Unique" Syndrome), *Nikkei* Newspaper, May 6, 1991.

19. C. Nakane, *Japanese Society* (Tokyo: Charles E. Tuttle, 1984).
20. R. M. Kanter, "Collaborative Advantage: Successful Partnerships Manage the Relationship, Not Just the Deal," *Harvard Business Review,* July–August 1994, p. 104.
21. Hofstede, *Cultures and Organizations,* p. 26.
22. Trompenaars, *Riding the Waves of Culture,* p. 6.
23. Mitsubishi Research Institute and N. Makino, eds., *Gaishikei Kigyo ni manabu seikou senryaku* (Lessons from Best Run Foreign Companies Operated in Japan) (Tokyo: President, 1995), pp. 72–73.
24. Mitsubishi Research Institute and N. Makino, eds., *Gaishikei Kigyo ni manabu seikou senryaku,* pp. 72–73.
25. T. Peters, *The Tom Peters Seminars: Crazy Times Call for Crazy Organizations* (New York: Vintage Books, 1994), p. 186.

Chapter Eight

1. R. T. Pascale, *Managing on the Edge: How the Smartest Companies Use Conflict to Stay Ahead* (New York: Simon & Schuster, 1990), p. 263.
2. W. Taylor, "The Logic of Global Business: An Interview with ABB's Percy Barnevik," *Harvard Business Review,* March–April 1991, p. 95.
3. P.A.L. Evans and Y. Doz, "Dualities: A Paradigm for Human Resource and Organizational Development in Complex Multinationals," in V. Pucik, N. M. Tichy, and C. Barnett, eds., *Globalizing Management: Creating and Leading the Competitive Organization* (New York: Wiley, 1992), p. 92.
4. R. T. Moran and J. R. Riesenberger, *The Global Challenge: Building the New Worldwide Enterprise* (Maidenhead, Berkshire, U.K.: McGraw-Hill, 1994), pp. 119–120.
5. I was inspired by many leading thinkers, including Paul A. L. Evans, Yves Doz, Ikujiro Nonaka, Kichiro Hayashi, and Michael Ray.
6. Pascale, *Managing on the Edge,* p. 14.
7. Evans and Doz, "Dualities," pp. 87–92.
8. Evans and Doz, "Dualities," pp. 87–92.
9. F. Trompenaars, *Riding the Waves of Culture: Understanding Diversity in Global Business,* rev. ed. (Burn Ridge, Ill.: Irwin Professional Publishing, 1994), p. 56.
10. Trompenaars, *Riding the Wave of Culture,* p. 55.
11. Evans and Doz, "Dualities," p. 87.
12. K. Hayashi, *Ibunka Interface Keiei* (Intercultural Management) (Tokyo: Nihon Keizai Shinbunsha, 1994), p. 141.
13. Hayashi, *Ibunka Interface Keiei,* pp. 141–142.
14. N. M. Tichy, "Global Development," in V. Pucik, N. M. Tichy, and C. K. Barnett, eds., *Globalizing Management: Creating and Leading the Competitive Organization* (New York: Wiley, 1992), pp. 210–211.

15. C. Bartlett and S. Ghoshal, "Matrix Management: Not a Structure, a Frame of Mind," *Harvard Business Review,* July–August 1990, p. 140.
16. F. Capra, "A System Approach to the Emerging Paradigm," in M. Ray and A. Rinzler, eds., *The New Paradigm in Business* (Los Angeles: Tarcher, 1993), pp. 231–232.
17. D. Chopra, *Quantum Healing Workshop* [audiotape] (New York: Sound Horizon Audio Video, 1990).
18. G. Hamel and C. K. Prahalad, "Strategic Intent," *Harvard Business Review,* May–June 1989.
19. Hamel and Prahalad, "Strategic Intent."
20. Capra, "A System Approach to the Emerging Paradigm," p. 232.
21. Tichy, "Global Development," p. 211.
22. M. Ray and R. Myers, *Creativity in Business* (New York: Doubleday, 1986), p. 195.
23. Pascale, *Managing on the Edge,* p. 18.
24. "Shifting Gears: Some American Manufacturers Drop Ill-Starred Efforts to Adopt Japanese Techniques," *Wall Street Journal,* May 7, 1993.
25. M. Ferguson, "The Transformation of Values and Vocation," in M. Ray and A. Rinzler, eds., *The New Paradigm in Business* (Los Angeles: Tarcher, 1993), p. 33.
26. "Reengineering the MBA," *Fortune,* January 24, 1994.
27. "Rienjiniaringu Kakumei" (Reengineering Revolution) (Tokyo: Nihon Keizai Shinbunsha, 1993), pp. 329–330. Translation of M. Hammer and J. Champy, *Reengineering the Corporation: A Manifesto for Business Revolution* (New York: HarperCollins, 1993).
28. I. Nonaka, "The Knowledge-Creating Company," *Harvard Business Review,* November–December 1991, p. 96.
29. I. Nonaka, "Rienjiniaringu wo koete" (Beyond Reengineering), *Nikkei* Newspaper, January 21, 1994.
30. Nonaka, "The Knowledge-Creating Company," p. 98.
31. Nonaka, "The Knowledge-Creating Company," p. 98.
32. Nonaka, "The Knowledge-Creating Company," p. 98.
33. Nonaka, "The Knowledge-Creating Company," pp. 98–99.
34. Nonaka, "The Knowledge-Creating Company," pp. 98–99.
35. B. Bernstein, "Elaborated and Restricted Codes: Their Social Origins and Some Consequences," in A. G. Smith, ed., *Communication and Culture: Readings in the Codes of Human Interaction* (Austin, Tex.: Holt, Rinehart and Winston, 1966).
36. Bernstein, "Elaborated and Restricted Codes, p. 437.
37. Hayashi, *Ibunka Interface Keiei,* pp. 129–140.
38. Hayashi, *Ibunka Interface Keiei,* p. 138.
39. "HR Facilitates the Learning Organization Concept," *Personnel Journal,* November 1994, p. 59.

40. P. Senge, *The Fifth Discipline: The Art and Practice of the Learning Organization* (New York: Doubleday Currency, 1990), pp. 73–74.
41. "HR Facilitates the Learning Organization Concept," p. 56.
42. Senge, *The Fifth Discipline,* p. 35.
43. G. Funakoshi, *Karate-Do My Way of Life* (Tokyo: Kodansha International, 1975), p. 101.

Chapter Nine

1. J. Naisbitt, *Megatrends* (New York: Warner Books, 1982), p. 76.
2. J. E. Rehfeld, "What Working for a Japanese Company Taught Me," *Harvard Business Review,* November–December 1990, p. 171.
3. Rehfeld, "What Working for a Japanese Company Taught Me," p. 171.
4. "When in Japan, Recruit as the Japanese Do—Aggressively," *Business Week,* June 24, 1991, p. 58.
5. "The Fast Track Now Leads Overseas," *U.S. News & World Report,* October 31, 1994, p. 98.
6. Y. Tsurumi, *Nihon Kigyo no Higeki* (Tragedy of Japanese Corporations) (Tokyo: Kobunsha, 1992), pp. 125–127.
7. N. J. Adler, *International Dimensions of Organizational Behavior* (Boston: Kent, 1991), pp. 134–135.
8. Adler, *International Dimensions of Organizational Behavior,* pp. 134–135.
9. Adler, *International Dimensions of Organizational Behavior,* pp. 139–141.
10. Adler, *International Dimensions of Organizational Behavior,* p. 58.

Chapter Ten

1. J. C. Abegglen and G. Stalk, Jr., *Kaisha: The Japanese Corporation* (New York: Basic Books, 1985), p. 241.
2. I. Kojima, *Gaishikei kigyou no keiretsu to seiryoku chizu* (Foreign-Capital Company at a Glance: Its Group and Strategic Position) (Tokyo: Nihon Jitsugyo Shuppansha, 1992), pp. 28–29.
3. M. Atarashi, *Kokusai Business ni tsuyoku naru hou* (Developing an International Business Sense: Honing Your International Business Skills) (Tokyo: PHP Institute, 1993), pp. 120–121.
4. Atarashi, *Kokusai Business ni tsuyoku naru hou,* pp. 120–121.
5. McKinsey & Co. and K. Ohmae, eds., *Boderless Jidai no Keiei Senryaku* (Strategy for the Borderless Age) (Tokyo: President, 1992), pp. 47–49.
6. R. Ohtaki, "Zainihichi Gaishi Kigyo-Chuchoki no Jinji Senryaku ni Fubi" (Foreign Capital Companies: Lack of Mid–Long Term Human Resources Strategy), *Nikkei* Newspaper, April 11, 1990.
7. G. Hofstede, *Cultures and Organizations: Software of the Mind* (Maidenhead, Berkshire, U.K.: McGraw-Hill, 1991), p. 113.

8. J. Duck, "Managing Change: The Art of Balancing," *Harvard Business Review,* November–December, 1993, p. 110.

9. P.-O. Berg, "Organization Change as a Symbolic Transformation Process," in P. J. Frost, ed., *Organizational Culture,* 5th printing (Thousand Oaks, Calif.: Sage, 1985), p. 298.

10. Mitsubishi Research Institute and N. Makino, ed., *Senryaku Kakushin Note* (Management Manual for Strategic Innovation) (Tokyo: President, 1992), pp. 32–42.

11. For example, W. Ouchi, *Theory Z: How American Business Can Meet the Japanese Challenge* (New York: Avon Books, 1981); and R. T. Pascale and A. G. Athos, *The Art of Japanese Management* (New York: Simon and Schuster, 1981).

Chapter Eleven

1. A. Toffler, *Power Shift: Knowledge, Wealth, and Violence at the Edge of the Twenty-First Century* (New York: Bantam Books, 1990), p. 428.

2. "Yomigaere seizogyo: Data de miru jyoshiki no uso" (Rebirth of Manufacturers: Data Shows the Inaccuracy of Common Sense), *Nikkei* Newspaper, January 11, 1994.

3. McKinsey & Co. and K. Ohmae, eds., *Boderless Jidai no Keiei Senryaku* (Strategy for the Borderless Age) (Tokyo: President, 1992), p. 144.

4. V. Pucik, M. Hanada, and G. Fifield, *Management Culture and the Effectiveness of Local Executives in Japanese-Owned U.S. Corporations* (Ann Arbor: Regents of The University of Michigan, 1989), pp. 19–21.

5. Pucik, Hanada, and Fifield, *Management Culture and the Effectiveness of Local Executives in Japanese-Owned U.S. Corporations,* pp. 19–21.

6. T. Amako, *Nihonjin Manager* (The Japanese Manager) (Osaka: Sogensha, 1992), pp. 189–199.

7. K. Hayashi, *Ibunka Interface Keiei* (Intercultural Management) (Tokyo: Nihon Keizai Shinbunsha, 1994), p. 40.

8. Mitsubishi Research Institute and N. Makino, ed., *Nihon Kigyo no Global Senryaku* (The Global Strategy of Japanese Corporations) (Tokyo: Diamond, 1992), pp. 19–21.

9. C. Bartlett and H. Yoshikawa, "New Challenges for Japanese Multinationals," in P. Lorange, ed., *Human Resource Management, 27*(1) (New York: Wiley, 1988), pp. 19–43.

10. "Nissan: Sunny Mo Beikoku Ikan" (Nissan: Transferring Sentra to the U.S.), *Nikkei* Newspaper, January 13, 1994.

11. "Nihon No Jinko, 2007 Nen Peak Ni Gensho" (Japanese Population Will Hit the Peak at 2007, and Thereafter Decrease), *Nikkei* Newspaper (evening edition), January 21, 1997.

12. "Nihongata Keiei ga abunai," *Bungei shunjyu,* February 1992, pp. 94–103.

13. S. Hori, "Fixing Japan's White Collar Economy: A Personal View," *Harvard Business Review,* November–December 1993, pp. 157–172.
14. *Nikkei* Newspaper, April 24, 1994.
15. "Ishin-denshin wa mou tsuujinai" (Tacit Understanding Does Not Work Anymore), *Nikkei* Newspaper, July 26, 1993.
16. Toffler, *Power Shift.*
17. "Trashing Tradition: Maverick Companies in Japan Begin to Change Ways of Doing Business There," *Wall Street Journal,* April 29, 1994.
18. Hayashi, *Ibunka Interface Keiei,* p. 183.
19. For example, Kichiro Hayashi at Aoyama Gakuin and Haruo Shimada at Keio University.
20. *Nikkei* Newspaper, March 1, 1996.

Chapter Twelve
1. Monsanto–Mitsubishi Kasei terminated their forty years of joint venture relationship. See "Gaishi-kei: Risutora tainichi senryaku" (Foreign Capital Company: Restructuring Strategy), *Nikkei* Newspaper, November 12, 1993; Borden–Meiji Milk Products, Unilever–Shin Oji Seishi, Cargil–Showa Sangyo, Anheiser Busch–Suntory also terminated. See "Gaishi-kei Shokuhin Maker Aitsugu 'Enkiri'" (Divorce Rush of Foreign Capital Companies), *Nikkei* Newspaper, November 25, 1993.
2. *Nikkei* Newspaper, November 25, 1993.
3. Aurthur D. Little and Y. Yamashita, *Senryaku Sanbo Map* (The Map for Strategists) (Tokyo: Diamond, 1991), p. 93.
4. K. Ohmae, *The Borderless World* (New York: Harper Business, 1990), p. 115.
5. S. C. Schneider, "National vs. Corporate Culture: Implications for Human Resource Management," in P. Lorange, ed., *Human Resource Management, 27*(1) (New York: Wiley, 1986), pp. 133–148.
6. Interview with Masazumi Ishii, March 9, 1995.
7. H. Perlmutter and D. Heenan, "Cooperate to Compete Globally," *Harvard Business Review,* March–April 1986; also in P. Barnevik, *Global Strategies: Insights from the World's Leading Thinkers,* (Boston: Harvard Business School Press, 1994), pp. 135–140.
8. V. Pucik, "Strategic Alliances, Organizational Learning, and Competitive Advantage: The HRM Agenda," in P. Lorange, ed., *Human Resource Management, 27*(1) (New York: Wiley, 1988), p. 80.
9. "Side by Side: Clash of Cultures Hobbles Joint Research Effort," *Wall Street Journal,* May 3, 1994.
10. V. Pucik, "Strategic Alliances, Organizational Learning, and Competitive Advantage: The HRM Agenda," pp. 77–93.

11. N. J. Adler, *International Dimensions of Organizational Behavior* (Boston: Kent, 1991), pp. 227–228.
12. N. M. Tichy, M. I. Brimm, R. Charan, and H. Takeuchi, "Leadership Development as a Lever for Global Transformation," in V. Pucik, N. M. Tichy, and C. Barnett, eds., *Globalizing Management: Creating and Leading the Competitive Organization* (New York: Wiley, 1993), pp. 51–55.
13. Egon-Zender and University of Michigan, *Zaibei Nikkei kigyo no Keiei bunka to genchi jyoukyu shain no katsuyou* (Tokyo: Egon-Zender, 1990), p. 73.
14. N. Phillips, *Managing International Teams* (Burr Ridge, Ill.: Irwin Professional, 1994), pp. 124–128.
15. Phillips, *Managing International Teams*, p. 128.
16. "How to Make a Merger Work," *Fortune*, January 24, 1994, p. 66.
17. P.-O. Berg, "Organization Change as a Symbolic Transformation Process," in P. J. Frost, ed., *Organizational Culture*, 5th printing (Thousand Oaks, Calif.: Sage, 1985), p. 298.

Chapter Thirteen

1. Although there are many books about Manjiro and Hikozo, I referred to K. Plummer, *The First Japanese to America* (Tokyo: NHK, 1989).
2. Estimated numbers calculated from Japan External Trade and Research Organization (JETRO), *U.S. and Japan in Figures* (Tokyo: Author, 1990).
3. J. S. Black, H. B. Gregersen, and M. E. Mendenhall, *Global Assignments: Successfully Expatriating and Repatriating International Managers* (San Francisco: Jossey-Bass, 1992), p. 14.
4. Black, Gregersen, and Mendenhall, *Global Assignments*, p. 76.
5. Lippitt and Lippitt (1975), described in W. W. Burke, *Organization Development: A Process of Learning and Changing* (Reading, Mass.: Addison-Wesley, 1994), p. 174.

Chapter Fourteen

1. D. Chopra, *Quantum Healing Workshop* [audiotape] (New York: Sound Horizon Audio Video, 1990).
2. B. Davis, "Global Paradox: World's Trade Binds Nations, But Can Split Them," *Wall Street Journal*, June 20, 1994.
3. "Borderless or Borderful," *Sapio*, April 11, 1991, pp. 84–89.
4. J. Naisbitt, *Megatrends* (New York, Warner Books, 1982), p. 76.
5. "Global Delusion," *International Business*, May 1995, pp. 14–15.
6. "The Discreet Charm of the Multicultural Multinational," *The Economist*, July 30, 1994, pp. 57–58.

7. Naisbitt, *Megatrends,* p. 76.
8. "Diversity Rears Its Head, Few Heed It," *New York Times,* November 13, 1994.
9. "Diversity Rears Its Head, Few Heed It."
10. "International Gurus: Teaching Big Business About Foreign Cultures Is Big Business Itself," *Wall Street Journal,* June 2, 1993.
11. A. P. Carnevale and S. C. Stone, "Diversity Beyond the Golden Rule," *Training & Development,* October 1994, p. 24.
12. Adapted from S. Tsuboi, *The Gokui* (The Essence of Martial Arts) (Tokyo: Chobunsha, 1973), pp. 147–152.
13. Confucian Analects 2:11.
14. H. Nakano, *Hegel* (Tokyo: Chuo-Koron, 1968), pp. 183–185.
15. P. Senge, *The Fifth Discipline: The Art and Practice of the Learning Organization* (New York: Doubleday Currency, 1990), pp. 284–285.
16. G. Hamel and C. K. Prahalad, *Competing for the Future* (Boston: Harvard Business School Press, 1994), pp. 59–60.
17. K. Nishida, *Zen no Kenkyu* (A Study of Goodness) (Tokyo: Iwanami, 1950), pp. 210–213.
18. Hamel and Prahalad, *Competing for the Future,* p. 60.
19. Nishida, *Zen no Kenkyu,* pp. 13–21.
20. T. Imahori and W. Cupack, "Identity Management Theory," in R. L. Wiseman and J. Koester, eds., *Intercultural Communication Competence* (Thousand Oaks, Calif.: Sage, 1991), pp. 112–131.
21. Wiseman and Koester, eds., *Intercultural Communication Competence,* pp. 112–131.
22. Wiseman and Koester, eds., *Intercultural Communication Competence,* pp. 112–131.
23. Imahori and Cupack, "Identity Management Theory," p. 129.

Index

A

Abegglen, J., 136

Achieved status, 87

Action learning, compressed, 45–46

Adler, N. J., 14–15, 23, 57, 131–132

Agape, 192–194

Aikido, 192

Alliances. *See* United States–Japan alliances

Ambiguity toleration, 76–77. *See also* Uncertainty avoidance

American communication, 24–25, 83–84; as low-context/high-content, 85. *See also* Communication; Cultural context; Culture. *See also United States headings*

American companies: learning organization model of, 116–119; transformation of, from low-to high-context management, 113. *See also United States headings*

American companies in Japan (*gaishi*), 18–19, 136–149; change management in, 143–148; contextual literacy for, 148–149; cross-cultural mismanagement in, case scenario, 3–5; customer satisfaction and, 137; difficulties of, 136–137; diversity management in, 187–188; glass ceilings in, 128; headquarters-Japanese operations relationship and, 137–139, 141–143; human resource issues of, 142–143; intervention for, 197–199; Japanese middle managers in, 147; Japanese students' preference for, 126; major concerns of managers of, 136–139; problems of, common to Japanese companies, 125–130; recruitment problems of, 125–126, 142–143; success factors of, 137, 138; vicious cycle of management of, 141–143. *See also* Change management; Headquarters-regional office relationship; United States–Japan alliances; United States–Japan cross-cultural business environment

American Graduate School of International Management, 55, 128, 152

American International Group (AIG), 24–25, 182

American management experts/management research: and cultural context, 87–88, 146–147; cross-cultural impediments of, 22–25, 146–147; information gap in, 123–124, 136

American management practices: applicability of, to other cultures, 91, 95; attempts to synthesize Japanese techniques with, 104–105, 109–110; and leadership behaviors, 18–19, 23. *See also* Cross-cultural management; *United States headings*

American managers: Japanese managers' frustration with, 124; major concerns of, 136–139. *See also United States headings*

American mindset map, 69

217